What Would Jesus Post?

The Bible Reading Fellowship
15 The Chambers, Vineyard
Abingdon OX14 3FE
brf.org.uk

The Bible Reading Fellowship (BRF) is a Registered Charity (233280)

ISBN 978 0 85746 664 8
First published 2018
10 9 8 7 6 5 4 3 2 1 0
All rights reserved

Text © David J. Robertson 2018
This edition © The Bible Reading Fellowship 2018
Cover image © John Lamb/Getty Images; Bible text photograph by Rebecca J Hall

The author asserts the moral right to be identified as the author of this work

Acknowledgements
Scripture quotations are taken from The Holy Bible, New International Version
(Anglicised edition) copyright © 1979, 1984, 2011 by Biblica. Used by permission of
Hodder & Stoughton Publishers, a Hachette UK company. All rights reserved. 'NIV' is a
registered trademark of Biblica. UK trademark number 1448790.

Every effort has been made to trace and contact copyright owners for material used
in this resource. We apologise for any inadvertent omissions or errors, and would
ask those concerned to contact us so that full acknowledgement can be made in
the future.

A catalogue record for this book is available from the British Library

Printed and bound by CPI Group (UK) Ltd, Croydon CR0 4YY

DAVID ROBERTSON

What Would Jesus Post?

A **BIBLICAL** approach to **ONLINE INTERACTION**

Contents

Foreword

Christians are called by Jesus himself to be salt and light in a complex world. The thing about salt is that, as a refrigerant or fertiliser (in first-century Palestine), it gets absorbed by the meat or soil and loses its identity; it gives up its life for the sake of that to which it is committed.

But, how does this apply to a world now dominated by the internet with all its promise and threat? How should Christians get stuck in to a world of communication over which they have little control, but from which they cannot afford to withdraw? What might it mean for Christians to shed light in a medium that gives licence to a massive amount of darkness?

The first thing to note is that Jesus cared less about his own 'cleanliness' than he did about contaminating his world with grace, generosity, honesty, mercy and love. If he didn't worry about getting dirty, then neither should his people. This is a relief because engagement with the online world is not a precise art, and cannot be controlled. Getting stuck in means taking a risk, learning from mistakes and exploring opportunities as well as questioning challenges.

The second thing to note is that the key to online engagement is the recognition that it involves conversation rather than preaching. If you preach a monologue, you will find only the converted listening online; conversation invites challenge, dispute and hearing views we might not like. But, that's the nature of the beast, and we should not kid ourselves that we are being heard just because we have said or written something.

All of this underlies this helpful book. Rather than urging that good Christians shun a frequently dodgy medium, David Robertson offers straightforward and wise advice for those who wish to reflect on what Christian engagement looks like. 'Humble, hospitable and generous' is more than the title of a chapter; it summarises what Robertson wants to encourage. Every individual will need to work out what their engagement might look like, but this book offers some guidelines for keeping us generally on track.

Rt Revd Nicholas Baines
Bishop of Leeds

Introduction

The way it is

The idea of the internet as a network, or 'web', of connected computers all using the same 'protocols' to communicate with each other (regardless of the different software being run on each machine) was first developed in the 1960s. Tim Berners-Lee created the World Wide Web as we know it in 1990, and in 1995 the first Internet Service Providers (ISPs) made it accessible to the general public. By 2010, it had become ubiquitous in every aspect of contemporary life – so, in a few short years the internet changed… well, what?

The world? No.

Before the internet, the world was a mixture of the great, the good, the indifferent, the bad and the ugly. The internet has changed the way in which human beings access the world and contact each other, but the technology (tech) has not created a utopia. The world is the same as it always has been and the internet reflects this. Go online and you will find that the great, the good, the indifferent, the bad and the ugly are all just one click away.

Because of the rapid development of the internet, we live in a broadly three-generational tech-culture. The older generation are 'tech-immigrants', many of whom don't speak the language of the new 'online land', still prefer to operate in the 'offline' culture of their past and think in the 'offline language' of their earlier years. The middle generation are 'tech-assimilators' who have integrated into the online land, language and culture (which they understand and appreciate, and can interpret for the older generation). The younger generation are 'indigenous' to the online land; it is where they live, how they think and their culture. This three-generational tech-culture is neither race- nor language-dependent, and while there are individual exceptions with cross-generational tech-attitudes, it applies generally to every nation, neighbourhood and family on the planet.

The question for Christian people is, in an online age, regardless of the generation to which we belong, which biblical principles shape our approach to online interaction?

Digging deeper

The majority of British people will answer that question with another: 'Why would the Bible have *anything* to say about the internet?' After all, the Bible is a collection of ancient books and the internet is brand-new tech! How could the one be of any possible relevance to the other? Those same people, however, will access the world through the web, stare at their screens in horror and ask, 'Why are people so horrible to each other? Why can't everyone just be nice?' At that point, they have just asked two of the most basic questions that exist – and the Bible not only answers them, it offers a solution that changes everything.

Paul wrote: 'All scripture is God-breathed and is useful for teaching, rebuking, correcting and training in righteousness, so that the servant of God may be thoroughly equipped for every good work' (2 Timothy 3:16–17). The way human beings access information, products and services through the internet is constantly developing. The way we connect with each other and interact online has been transformed. Yet none of this has made any fundamental changes to human beings. We remain with our hopes, fears, aspirations, talents, flaws... (and the list goes on).

New tech never changes people per se, and history shows that it offers both opportunities and consequences. For example, developments in transport, industry, printing, communications, media (you name it) have all provided opportunities, but have also come with consequences (such as the increasing global rich/poor divide and environmental pollution). Neither steam trains nor paperback books intrinsically changed human beings, but the opportunities they provided did, and in every age, Christians have reflected on new tech and asked, 'How can we approach this new opportunity in a way that honours God and affirms others?' The answer, of course, has been through a biblical approach, allowing the 'God-breathed' scriptures to address the human condition which bubbles away under, and through, the tech.

Pause for thought

If Jesus had access to the internet, what would he post? His parables? His sharp observations on hypocrisy? No one can say, but we can guess what he would share or retweet. He regularly quoted the scriptures, so the psalms would no doubt figure in his online feed. More than this, though, Jesus was 'God with us' (Matthew 1:22–23), which, in online jargon, means: God's self-post to the world; God's post-made-flesh; and he not only retweeted the scriptures, he inhabited them and fulfilled them (Matthew 26:56). What would Jesus post? The words behind the title on the cover of this book are there for a reason (Psalm 78:1–4).

Joining the dots

The internet exists only while computers are switched on. If power stations run out of sustainable fuel, and the electricity supply fails, so does the internet. If the natural resources needed to manufacture online devices are mined to exhaustion (for example, the silicone used for chips, the gold used for electrical connections on circuit boards, the lithium used to make batteries, and the indium used to coat touchscreens) the internet stops. The internet may appear to have a life which is independent from elements dug from the soil, but it doesn't; in the sense that for it to exist it must consume the earth's resources, it isn't 'free'. For the near future, however, it is likely to remain and, providing new tech-elements replace those which are being consumed (and running out), our great-great-great grandchildren will connect online too.

It may be helpful for those who are hazy about the internet to understand it as a 'land' or a 'town' which has:

- **Roads**. These are provided by Internet Service Providers (ISPs). Most people pay for 'toll-road access' by signing a contract, paying a monthly fee and using the router their ISP sends them to 'get them on the road'. Some people sign up for 'free' ISP access (providing they are happy to be advertised to all the time). Without an ISP, you won't be going anywhere on the internet, but once you are online, where you go is up to you, and search engines are like satnavs which direct you to the places you want to visit.

- **Private addresses**. These are personal 'locations' on the internet and you will have one or more address. It's where you 'live' online, and where you can be contacted.

- **Shops**. You can visit, browse, buy things, ask for clarification, talk to other customers (by reading their reviews and asking them questions), complain and generally interact.

- **Entertainment**. Where you go to watch movies, listen to music, read books and so forth.

- **Communications**. These include 'post boxes' for sending digital letters and 'phone boxes' for making digital phone calls.

- **Community spaces**. Online 'chat rooms' still exist where people can discuss issues or make friends in real time, but mostly, social media now provides both 'real-time' and 'when convenient' interaction.

- **Billboards**. These tend to be amateur websites (for example, church websites) which advertise their services and provide contact details. Like billboards by the roadside, you can look at what's on offer, but you can't go in and shop or interact; if you want to make contact, you have to 'write' or 'phone'.

- **A marketplace**. The online 'open arena' is the contemporary equivalent of the first-century 'marketplace' and it can be very busy, noisy, shouty and even scary.

A fundamental concept to understand is that the internet itself has no 'content' (any more than TV aerials contain programmes) and that every single 'place' on the internet is a website. When you are online, you are not looking at 'the internet', you are viewing a series of websites:

- Amazon, eBay, Ocado, the supermarkets, the banks, and *millions* more, are all websites. They are complex, professional websites, but they are still just websites.
- Google, Bing, Yahoo, Ask (and all search engines) – websites again.
- Netflix, iTunes, on-demand TV and all the entertainment providers – they are websites too.
- ISPs (BT, Sky, Virgin, TalkTalk and the rest) are accessed through their websites.
- Gmail, Skype and all the other email, texting, messaging and video-call facilitators – websites.
- Facebook, Twitter, Pinterest, Reddit, Flickr (and the plethora of social media sites) are all websites as well, just like your personal blog or your church website is a website.

Every single time you look at your device screen, you connect to a website of one kind or another. To express it at its most basic, imagine that your computer screen has two sides; you look through the front of yours, but your screen is connected back-to-back to someone else's; you look through your screen into theirs, and they look through their screen into yours.

Only the protocols which allow the internet to function are fixed points. Websites come and go and, while the major sites are likely to develop and remain, no website is eternal. Similarly, the devices we use to access the internet change over time. At the moment, we use desktop computers, laptops, tablets and smartphones to interact online, but that will no doubt change as new tech becomes available. While tech and websites come and go, however, the biblical principles which help us to steward our online interactions remain. They do not change – and *they* are the focus of this book. Resources abound to help those who wish to develop a church website or social media page, setting up profiles, privacy options, along with really useful, practical advice about dealing with technical difficulties[1] – but these matters are not the subject of this book. Here, the focus is not on the tech that allows us to interact, nor on the websites through which we interact, but on the people with whom we interact personally, and on how Christians might approach that interaction from a biblical direction.

A way forward

You can read this book, if you wish, by 'dipping in' and reading the chapters in order of your interest, but be aware that the early chapters inform those that come later, and later chapters make more sense once the principles outlined in earlier chapters have been considered. Having said that, every chapter follows the same pattern, with the same headings:

- **The way it is**: outlines a particular issue or challenge.

- **Digging deeper**: considers a biblical understanding of the issue or challenge.

- **Joining the dots**: links the issue or challenge with either practical 'real-world' consequences, the overall biblical thinking, or with both.

- **A way forward**: points towards attitudes and behaviour that can encourage a biblical approach.

- **Pause for thought**: (which can appear under any heading) gives a different perspective to encourage reflection, discussion and a deeper understanding. In a teaching series, these could be used as illustrations.

- **The biblical principle**: suggests a Bible passage which expresses the biblical insight. The main topic of this book is the personal stewardship of online interaction, and biblical quotations are included throughout. Other biblical understandings contribute to this 'main stream', though, and further references nod in the direction of these related topics. You can read this book without pursuing any of them, or you can use them for further Bible study.[2]

- **Wisdom from the Psalms**: can be used for personal reflection, group prayer, or the basis of a liturgical response.

- **Some questions to think about**: can be used for personal reflection, group discussion or suggestions for practical application.

The intention is for this book to be as flexible as possible. Individuals can use it to think through their personal online interaction; parents and youth leaders can use it to help children and young people; groups can use it as a study aid; and church leaders can use it as a resource.

The sectional approach in each chapter also allows for easy revisiting. For example, if you want to go back and focus on the theology, head for the 'Digging deeper' section of each chapter; if it's the practical applications that are of most interest, go to 'A way forward'; if it's a resource for devotional material you are after, go to 'Wisdom from the Psalms'. Just be aware that reading each chapter in order will give the most rounded understanding of a biblical approach to online interaction, and the sectional approach within each chapter is intended to help those who wish to use this book as a resource as they develop their own programmes directly suited to their local or personal situation.

And finally, before we move on to Chapter 1, we need to define terms. While some websites use the same jargon, others use their own. Depending on the sites you use (especially when it comes to social media):

- **You may be a**: customer, member, user, contact, friend, follower, pinner, circle (and who knows what else).

- **You will either**: post, tweet, pin, publish, snap; share, retweet, network; like, note, +1, follow, reblog, connect; comment, message, tag, hashtag (and that's before you invite, stumble, upvote, dislike or story).

Clearly, within the covers of this book, terms need to be agreed, otherwise, on each occasion, a whole list has to be used. Although Facebook and Twitter have coined the most ubiquitous terms, this book is not partisan in any way, so the terms used in the following pages will be as neutral as possible and not suggest a connection to any single company or website:

- **Post** means: add content, tweet, pin, publish, snap...
- **Circulate** means: share, retweet, network...
- **Approve** means: like, note, endorse...
- **Remark** means: comment; reply...
- **Message** means: mail, email, message, text...
- And... rather than using terms such as 'physical world' and 'virtual world' (or similar) the terms 'offline life' and 'online life' will usually be used. This puts the focus on the life, rather than on the 'world', and makes it clear that our focus is personal rather than objective.

The biblical principle

> Do not conform to the pattern of this world, but be transformed
> by the renewing of your mind.
>
> ROMANS 12:2a

The internet provides a new opportunity to connect with other people, and leaves Christians with a choice – to be conformed to the online culture which, by default, has already established itself, or to look to God, through the transforming of our minds, and approach online life in a different way.

Wisdom from the Psalms

> The earth is the Lord's, and everything in it,
>   the world, and all who live in it.
>
> PSALM 24:1

Some questions to think about

1   Which tech-generation are you? What online issues are of most concern to you personally? What issues concern you most about the other two tech-generations' online lives?

2   Do you think that your online life has been conformed to the online world, or transformed by God's renewing of your mind? Have you asked God to do this?

3   Make a list of the websites you regularly visit and interact with, and reflect on opportunities you have taken and opportunities you know you have missed. At the beginning of this book, what is your hope for your online life?

1

Shouted from the online rooftops

The way it is

Picture the scene: you are invited to address your school or place of work. Actually, no; as well as every person in your school or workplace, it will be their friends and families too. At a prearranged time, they will all gather in one place, you will mount a platform, stand before them, and speak into a microphone. What will you say?

To imagine this scenario properly, perhaps it should begin with the question of preparation: how long would you need to prepare for this once-in-a-lifetime opportunity? How many drafts would you go through before you were satisfied with your final script? How many people would you ask for advice before you were confident that your words were worth listening to? Who would you ask to proofread your script, to warn you about insults or remark-bombs which had slipped through your own internal filters? How much prayer would you put into the whole enterprise?

The day comes, you climb up to the platform, you approach the microphone, you peer nervously at the sea of faces in front of you, and what do you do? Show them a picture of your lunch? Play a video of a kitten falling downstairs? Insult your head teacher or boss? Give everyone a photograph of your body parts? Of course not! This is a public event with a crowd of strangers! And yet day after day, week after week, people post the equivalent online.

In order to understand this phenomenon, it's helpful to understand the levels of trust within which human beings normally operate when interacting offline. Imagine that your home is surrounded by a large outer wall with a sturdy gate. Some visitors will be allowed through the gate but only as far as the front door. Some will be welcomed into your house but only into downstairs rooms. Only very close friends or family will be allowed upstairs, and even within the family there will probably be rules about who enters which bedroom and how (teenagers, for example, may be expected to knock on their parents' bedroom door before entering).

Now apply this image to your personal life and it represents different levels of trust. Some people are kept completely 'out', others are 'allowed in' – but how far will depend on the level of trust. When conversing with a stranger on a train, you may allow that person 'through the gate in your outer wall', but no further. (For example, you may share general information about your work and family, but no details or emotions, and the conversation is friendly, but distant.) Genuine friends may be allowed 'in through your front door' and close friends invited into your 'family spaces', but personal matters (upstairs confidences) will probably only be entrusted to your spouse or to a reliable confidant, and most people have secrets which are only whispered to God.

At some point, we have probably all met people who are so 'locked up' that they share nothing personal with anyone (not even with family members), and we have also probably met individuals who are so 'open' that they tell everyone *everything* (which can be equally difficult). Most people learn who to trust, and how much, as they grow up, but things still go wrong, and people misjudge others all the time. Sometimes, people believe a person to be trustworthy when they are not; spouses who divorce may use intimate knowledge to wound; and, to put it bluntly, people let others down and life can be hard. When it comes to online communication, however, everything posted has the potential to land beyond the 'outer wall', where it will be entirely visible to the scrutiny of the whole world. So how do so many people end up posting inappropriately personal content?

The answer is, apparently, 'Easily.' This may be, in part, a result of emotions driving actions (leading them to 'post in anger'), but generally it's because people forget the levels of trust they are so familiar with in their offline life. There are occasions when group chats, video conferencing (and such like) remind everyone that the World Wide Web is a public arena but, most of the time, to the user, it appears to be private. There may be other people in their offline vicinity (perhaps family members in the same room, colleagues in the office, or a crowd of strangers on a train), but although these people surround the user physically in the offline world, none of them takes part in the online conversation. The user is engaged with their device (their computer, tablet, phone and so forth), and to them, what they are posting feels as private as reading a book or writing a diary. This sense of privacy is, however, a deception, as even the most private and briefly expressed opinion may be mistakenly posted to a public forum. It can also be 'screen grabbed', or circulated by the recipient, and it totally ignores the fact that, while the user is focused on a single person or issue, they are on a website which is being hosted by a third party (which is looking back through their screen at them). They are actually alongside millions of other 'invisible' users on the same website who only need an invitation from someone involved in the conversation to join in! However private that content is to the user, the truth is, once the user hits the 'post' button (or equivalent), it is potentially public.

Everyone is aware of this, and yet the 'one-to-one' nature of the tech encourages forgetfulness to the extent that many people post in haste, repent at leisure and, increasingly, overstep the boundary between opinion and libel. Private prosecutions over inappropriate content are set to rise and, generally speaking, the problem is that the public nature of the internet has been misunderstood. To use the trust-level image already used, because the user is in their bedroom when they post, they think that it is appropriate to post a 'bedroom-level' remark, photo or video. Online, though, there *is* no guaranteed 'bedroom-level privacy'; everything posted potentially lands beyond the 'outer wall' where everyone can see it.

Consider a private email or message from one person to another, which is accessed through those two peoples' online devices. Leaving aside a malicious offline 'friend' or relative who 'borrows' either device, scrolls through it and reads the email without permission, the email does not exist only on those two devices. It will be scanned (for advertising purposes – which is why, if you mention that you are thinking of changing your laptop, ads for laptops appear on most websites you visit), and retained by both the email sender's and receiver's ISPs; deleting it will only make it invisible to the users. If the users are emailing or messaging through a website other than their ISPs, then a copy will be scanned and retained by that website too. There may also be other online hosts involved in passing it along – and all of them will scan it and keep a copy. Users may trust these companies, and the companies may be trustworthy, but if they are hacked, that oh-so-private email (and its details) can pop up anywhere. That, however, refers to general offline and online activity, where morality is often subjective to the individuals or to the companies involved. For Christians, there is an objective principle with which to steward this public aspect of our online presence.

Digging deeper

Christians are used to the idea of a 'future day of judgement'. Jesus' parable of the sheep and goats (Matthew 25:31–46) speaks of a throne of judgement before which the people of all nations will gather; Paul speaks of the judgement of believers (1 Corinthians 3:10–15); and the book of Revelation is filled with apocalyptic images. It is part of Jesus' teaching that judgement includes intentions as well as actions (Matthew 5:21–22, 27–28) and that nothing is secret from God:

> There is nothing concealed that will not be disclosed, or hidden
> that will not be made known. What you have said in the dark
> will be heard in the daylight, and what you have whispered in
> the ear in the inner rooms will be proclaimed from the roofs.
> LUKE 12:2–3

This kind of exposure is not just a future judgement, either; while
that awaits every person (even believers, whose judgement has
already been taken by Christ – Hebrews 9:27–28), judgement can
also be 'brought forward' to the here and now (Numbers 32:23).

For a Christian believer, everything is already public in the sense that
we expect God to be aware of everything that we do, say or think. Is it
so hard to remember that, when engaging with others online, every
post or remark, every opinion expressed, and everything approved
or circulated, is potentially visible to the scrutiny of the entire human
race?

Secular advice is that no one should post, circulate, approve, remark
on or send anything which they would not be happy to have read out
in a court of law. For Christians, though, there is a deeper question to
answer. Do our private words and opinions resonate with our public
proclamation of faith, or do the words we whisper in supposedly
private 'inner online rooms' reveal hypocrisy? Our social media
contributions in particular will make this clear.

Joining the dots

On a fundamental level, secrets being shouted from rooftops is very
good news. When a government official or religious leader is revealed
to have a seedy private life; or when an oppressive regime commits
an atrocity and then tries to hush it up; or when those trusted as
carers are revealed as abusers – such things *should* be shouted from
the rooftops. It's good that judgement does not always wait until
God's final judgement after death, and that wrongs committed in

this life can surface and be addressed. It does need to be recognised, however, that what applied in the offline past to governments, organisations and high-profile individuals, now also applies to anyone with an online presence; and it should be recognised that the internet is probably the worst place to confess or discuss anything personal. Christians should also expect to be subjected to close scrutiny. Just as a tree is known to be good or bad by its fruit (Luke 6:43–45), in the same way, in the 21st century, Christians are known to be good or bad not only by their actions in the offline world but by their online content.

Some Christians approach the judgement of God with confident trust, and some with a certain amount of trepidation, but if we are familiar with the idea that our inner sin will one day be shouted from the rooftops, then Christians, of all people, should be unsurprised when secret sin is revealed and bounced across the digital rooftops of the internet – especially when the information comes straight from the sinner!

Pause for thought

Even when you post wholesome content, you may receive an 'online outcry' for it. A major misquote was used as a core accusation at Jesus' trial (Mark 14:58; John 2:19–21), and Peter says: 'If you suffer for doing good and you endure it, this is commendable before God' (1 Peter 2:20b). If a loving and truthful remark leads to an online outcry, regard it as part of the cost of following Christ (1 Peter 2:21) and recognise the digital kicking for what it is (Matthew 5:11–12).

A way forward

Let's take a moment to consider the 'day of future judgement' when the words, actions, omissions and intentions of our entire life are scrutinised by God. Do we imagine that our online contributions or omissions will be, themselves, omitted or overlooked? To revisit the imaginary scenario at the beginning of this chapter (when we were given the opportunity to address so many people), have we squandered these opportunities? Have we used them to insult and hurt others? Have we participated in lies and libel by circulating information which, at the time, just seemed amusing? Do we think that God takes no view on what we post, circulate or approve online? If we understand judgement, we must conclude that our online presence is, like every other aspect of our lives, of interest to God.

- Scrutinise the content of others before you approve or circulate it. 'Let no one deceive you with empty words, for because of such things God's wrath comes on those who are disobedient' (Ephesians 5:6).

- Refuse to be drawn into mob rule. 'Have nothing to do with the fruitless deeds of darkness, but rather expose them' (Ephesians 5:11).

- Post positive words. 'Always giving thanks to God the Father for everything, in the name of our Lord Jesus Christ' (Ephesians 5:20).

The biblical principle

What you have said in the dark will be heard in the daylight, and what you have whispered in the ear in the inner rooms will be proclaimed from the roofs.
LUKE 12:3

- If you need to, write that verse on a Post-it note and stick it to your screen.

- And if you don't want your remarks to be shouted from the digital rooftops, don't even whisper them online... ever!

The offline expectation is that Christians will have Christ running through every aspect of their lives (Romans 5:1–6; 2 Corinthians 5:21). Do you imagine that the online expectation is any different?

Wisdom from the Psalms

If we had forgotten the name of our God
   or spread out our hands to a foreign god,
would not God have discovered it,
   since he knows the secrets of the heart?
PSALM 44:20–21

Some questions to think about

1 To what extent does the public nature of the internet impact the content you post or don't post? Do you vary the levels of trust depending on the online arena you are in (for example, social media, a discussion forum or a blog)?

2 If you engage in online debate (which might lead to significant contention), are there issues where it is more appropriate to remark as a group or a church, rather than as an individual?

3 Is there anything in your present or past online history which you should confess to God and maybe apologise to someone about?

2

Pray before posting

The way it is

Prayer is at the heart of Christian spirituality, and while some are gifted in prayer and others have to apply significant willpower to pray at all, most Christians are somewhere in between. Whatever our personal experience of prayer, though, we know that it connects us with God, and through prayer we seek to connect the whole of life with him. Prayer is not only at the heart of our spiritual lives, it is central to the whole of life. This is why Christians pray as individuals and together; we are connecting with God and offering ourselves to him, willing to be directed.

Paul says, 'Pray in the Spirit on all occasions with all kinds of prayers and requests' (Ephesians 6:18a). There are, therefore, no occasions when prayer is not appropriate – so where does it figure in your online life?

Digging deeper

Corporate prayer has a very long history and has always been relational. 'Look to the Lord and his strength; seek his face always' (1 Chronicles 16:11) sums up the Old Testament view of prayer; it's about talking with God. Human beings had a 'face-to-face' relationship with God in the garden of Eden (Genesis 2), but the Old Testament teaches that, even though the fall made that relationship distant (Genesis 3), prayer became the means through which God and people could still connect.

This prayer connection continues in the New Testament, where Jesus assumes that prayer is normal. For example, when he teaches the Lord's Prayer (Matthew 6:9–13), he begins by saying, '*When* you pray' (v. 5), not 'if', or 'should you feel like it'; he says 'when'. He assumes that prayer will be a regular part of his disciples' lives, and it clearly was, even though they struggled with it (for example, on one of the most important nights in history – Mark 14:32–42). After the resurrection of Jesus, and the coming of the Holy Spirit at Pentecost, prayer continued at the heart of the new church (Acts 2:42; 4:23–24; 12:12) and continues today. In the 21st century, in every country, when Christians meet, they pray.

Individual prayer is also important, and perhaps the best example of why is found in Mark 9:14–29. This incident takes place after the transfiguration (where Jesus, Peter, James and John have an extraordinary 'mountaintop' experience). While they are still up the mountain, down below, a father brings his possessed son to the remaining disciples. They attempt to heal the boy, but they fail and only make matters worse because, when Jesus arrives, the man is not even sure that Jesus can help (vv. 22–24). The man (rightly) expected Jesus' disciples to act under Jesus' authority and deliver the goods, but their failure causes him to doubt Jesus.

Jesus, however, heals the boy even though the boy's father must have thought it had all gone wrong (v. 26), and afterwards, the disciples ask Jesus why he could heal the boy when they couldn't. Jesus tells them, 'This kind can only come out with prayer' – which is a very odd answer, because the one thing Jesus didn't do was pray! He arrived, spoke to the boy's father, chastised his disciples for their lack of faith, asked about the boy, commanded him to be healed and handed him back to his father. When did he pray? The answer, of course, is on all those occasions when he went off by himself (Luke 5:16).

The inference is that regular, personal prayer is like jogging. It keeps us 'fit'. If you jog, then on the occasions when you need to run for a bus, you can. If you don't jog, you will miss the bus every time.

Jesus was a regular 'prayer jogger' but it seems likely that the disciples were not – and on this occasion, when the man brought his son for healing, Jesus was fit and the disciples weren't. In terms of interacting with others and with God, Jesus was the living equivalent of 'pray before posting'.

Joining the dots

The New Testament letters of Paul, Peter, John and James all refer to different aspects of prayer, and encourage Christians to use it to bring everything to God (Philippians 4:6). So, here's the challenge: when do you pray about your online life? If you already pray about the offline challenges and opportunities presented by each day, then surely it is only natural to pray about the challenges and opportunities online?

Pause for thought

If you interact online as soon as you wake up in the morning and only disengage when you fall asleep at night, at what point in the day do you take time out to pray? You may talk about God being your constant companion, but it may be chastening to keep a daily diary of how often you connect with God compared to how often you connect online. If your smartphone is your (real) constant companion, it may have taken the place of God – and that is idolatry.

Paul teaches, 'Do not conform to the pattern of this world, but be transformed by the renewing of your mind. Then you will be able to test and approve what God's will is – his good, pleasing and perfect will' (Romans 12:2). In other words, Christians are called to be countercultural. So, look at your online life and consider these three questions:

- Is your online presence indistinguishable from those with no faith? If it is, then probably, without even noticing it, you have been 'conformed to the pattern of this world'.

- Do you know God's will for your online life? If not, you have probably been 'conformed to the pattern of this world', where so much is posted that cannot, by any measure, be regarded as 'good, pleasing or perfect' by God's standard.

- Does your online life 'transform you by the renewing of your mind'? If not, then it is likely that your online life is disconnected from God. And how do we connect? Through prayer.

Whether or not we are conformed to this world, or transformed by God, will be directly influenced by how and what we pray. Our online 'agility' (knowing what to remark, how to respond and what to post) will have a direct correlation with our 'prayer jogging'. Jog and you get fit; don't jog and you will miss the bus every time.

A way forward

If, at this point, you are feeling challenged or guilty, don't beat yourself up! There is a reason why the Lord's Prayer contains the words, 'Lead us not into temptation, but deliver us from the evil one' (Matthew 6:13). Those words are not there by accident and they apply to our online life as much as to any other aspect of our lives.

Admittedly, when most churches address the subject of 'temptation', sexual temptation ranks high on the list, and the availability of internet pornography makes this dimension of online life a particular cause for concern (especially in the online lives of young people). It's easy to see why this happens and, to address this concern, the following chapter, 'A covenant with the eyes', is all about sex. Making anxiety about sex the top priority, though, misses the point that temptation abounds in *every* aspect of life and that falling into temptation without even noticing is easy. Avoiding sexual temptation online is the right thing to do – but if you assume that because you have avoided online sexual temptation everything else is hunky-dory, you are deceiving yourself (1 John 1:8). What about sharing in personal attack under the guise of humour? What about keeping quiet for fear of online reprisals? In order to fall into temptation, all we have to do is forget about God's 'good, pleasing and perfect will' and become so enamoured with what's in front of us that we never even consider that God has a view about whatever it is we are about to post (or not post). And... the best way to forget God is to forget to pray.

The heart of the matter is summed up by Paul: 'I sent to find out about your faith. I was afraid that in some way the tempter had tempted you and that our labours might have been in vain' (1 Thessalonians 3:5). Temptation to conform to the pattern of this world undoes the work of Christ in us. God's intention is for everyone to be a new creation, where the old has gone and the new is alive and well (2 Corinthians 5:17). The tempter's intention is to 'snatch away' (Matthew 13:19), and when that happens, the work God has done in transforming that life is undone.

So: pray before, during and after posting!

The biblical principle

> Pray in the Spirit on all occasions with all kinds of prayers and requests.
> EPHESIANS 6:18a

How can that apply to our online lives?

- Make sure that corporate prayer (when Christians gather on Sundays and in small groups) includes prayer about online challenges and opportunities.

- Get organised in personal daily prayer. Pray before you interact and trust the online day to come to God.

- Remember to let God in when online; think of your online interactions as a three-way conversation between you, God and others.

- Disengage before the end of the day and review your online day in prayer. Are there things to put right tomorrow? Anything to apologise for? Any opportunities to follow up?

Wisdom from the Psalms

Search me, O God, and know my heart;
   test me and know my anxious thoughts.
See if there is any offensive way in me,
   and lead me in the way everlasting.
PSALM 139:23–24

Some questions to think about

1 When was the last time your church, in a Sunday service, prayed about your church website or social media page? If this aspect of your church's life does not occupy any corporate prayer time, why not?

2 What proportion of your personal daily prayer is concerned with your online life? Do you pray about what others are posting? Do you ask God for guidance about who to connect with or how to remark? If not, why not?

3 Do you post without praying? Should you? Is there something practical you can do that will remind you to pray?

3

A covenant with the eyes

The way it is

It was noted in the previous chapter that online pornography (porn) causes anxiety in most churches, but it is important to understand that porn is not an isolated issue. Think of it as the edge of a coin. In Britain, we have a number of coins which are circular (with only one, continuous edge) but we also have three multi-edged coins (the 20p, 50p and £1 coins). Porn is one 'edge-section' of a multi-edged coin, and the other edge-sections include sexting, promiscuity, adultery, prostitution, sexual manipulation and so forth. They are part of the same 'coin' because they all share the same 'currency', which is lust, and just as British coins have the face of the monarch on them, the coin of lust has the face of its 'king' on it too – and it isn't the face of God, it's the face of the tempter.

It may appear, at first glance, that porn and prostitution are poles apart; but if you pay for porn, it is in the same direction as paying for sex. Porn might be differentiated from promiscuity, but both seek sex without a relationship. Similarly, viewing porn may appear to be different from adultery, but both redirect sexual desire away from the spouse. Porn may be regarded as 'sex at a distance' rather than physically personal, but it is one edge of a multi-edged coin where all the edges face into the same lustful centre.

Lust is named as one of the seven deadly sins, and it should therefore come as no surprise that it 'mixes' with other kinds of immorality. It is unsurprising that porn is a frequent bedfellow of criminality, the sex trade and broken lives, and while porn may appear (to some) to be harmless, those who seek it out online may well slide on to its 'neighbouring edges', or into life-changing criminal collusion. The internet is a public market; no one views anything in complete privacy (see Chapter 1), and week after week the police ring offline doorbells and arrest individuals who felt alone and safe when they browsed online.

Digging deeper

'I made a covenant with my eyes not to look lustfully at a young woman' (Job 31:1). The principle here is not about 'young women', but the lustful look (which could equally be directed towards any human being – of any age or gender). The point is that human eyes wander lustfully unless they are stopped by a covenant (a formal agreement with defined boundaries and commitments). In this case, the covenant is a deliberate agreement *not* to look.

Most New Testament passages about lust come from this same direction. Those who are serious about God should avoid lust because it is an area of life where Christians are either conformed to this world, or transformed by the Holy Spirit as part of the new life offered through Christ (1 John 2:15–17). Christians should flee from lust (1 Corinthians 6:18), because the end result is that, 'after desire has conceived, it gives birth to sin; and sin, when it is full-grown, gives birth to death' (James 1:15). Lust leads to sin against the sinner's own body and, since Christians have been bought by Christ and are indwelt by the Holy Spirit, what is done with those bodies matters (1 Corinthians 6:19–20; Ephesians 4:30). Lust, like any sin, pulls those who have received new life back into the old life – which is a life without Christ and therefore a place of death (separation from God).

In previous generations, fear of social exposure kept some people away from lust; others kept away out of a sense of duty to their spouse; others out of a desire to be obedient to God. All of these approaches came with a 'personal covenant', perhaps with society, with themselves, with their spouse or with God, and not a few of them led to double standards. In our own time, people want reasons, not duties, and that is maybe a good thing. So, the Bible teaches that lust is a sin… but why is lust, and in particular the edge we define as porn, a sin?

Joining the dots

The key which unlocks a proper view of porn is the Christian view of marriage, because the biblical assertion is that God's intention for sex is that it should express and build the marriage relationship. For a fuller understanding of marriage, have a look at my book about marriage,[3] but if we understand sex *within* marriage, then questions about porn tend to answer themselves.

According to Genesis (1:26, 28) a 'creation command' was given to human beings, which can be expressed as, 'Steward the earth, be blessed, and make babies.' This means that sex is part of God's created order and it should not, therefore, be a surprise that the human desire for sex is strong. God put it there. Human sin, however, led to the fall, and God's judgement put a block on that primary command (Genesis 3:16), which ensured that relationships without God would make human beings restless and ready to seek him. The judgement was, therefore, the ultimate 'for your own good' because it is only in seeking God that people find life.

Historically, Bible teachers taught that sex was *only* for making babies, but this ignored the text. The Bible recognises that sex is about more than procreation by its use of 'to know'. That sexual intimacy is described as 'knowing' reveals that human beings have a two-fold nature. Sex is a physical act, but it is also a spiritual joining. This is one dimension of what it means to be created in God's image and likeness (Genesis 1:26). God is a spiritual being who expresses himself physically, and we, physical beings, express ourselves spiritually. The physical act of sex has a spiritual dimension because, while the destination of sex is to unite body with body, the destination of love is to unite soul with soul. Making love is about the body expressing the soul, and the soul expressing the body.

Within marriage, the intention is that:

- A couple love each other, so they express their feelings sexually, and the sexual expression (which is physical) has spiritual content.

- The physical union brings a spiritual union, and the love between them is not only confirmed – it grows.

- They love each other, they express this sexually, this confirms and grows their love, so they express it sexually – and so on and so on.

That is a summary of sex within marriage from a Christian perspective; it expresses love, and builds love. It is like the glue between the past and the future, expressed in the present. Using this perspective as a lens, the reasons why promiscuity, adultery, prostitution (and so forth) are sins become clear. These are 'relationships' with no past and only a destructive future, and those who engage in them exchange the building of one sound relationship for a plethora of bits and pieces which litter the 'building site' of their lives and cause them, and others, to trip and fall. Lust is at the heart of it, and it is a sin that leads to 'death' (James 1:15).

What of porn, though? Most of the time it leads to no physical action with another person, so why is it on the same 'coin' as these other sinful actions? Because, although it is 'private', it is a matter of the heart. It may be 'further back' than physical sex, but it is in the same direction, and when Jesus speaks about the heart, he is very clear:

> You have heard that it was said, 'You shall not commit adultery.' But I tell you that anyone who looks at a woman lustfully has already committed adultery with her in his heart.
> MATTHEW 5:27–28

Again, the focus here is not on 'the woman' but on the heart that produces the lustful look – wherever it might alight.

Lust is like chickenpox; some people are covered in spots, others have very few, but the problem is the disease, not the spots. Compared to promiscuity, adultery and prostitution, looking at porn may not be regarded as a particularly 'spotty' expression of lust, but at its heart it's the same disease and it needs healing.

Pause for thought

Art seeks to ask questions of life; porn offers sexual gratification. If art, or porn, approach the 'boundary' that differentiates them, it may become difficult to tell which is which. However, in the vast majority of art works, or porn collections, the 'genre' is obvious. If in doubt, consider the artist's (or publisher's) other output; that will reveal the direction of their heart.

A way forward

Temptation and sin thrive in darkness, so haul porn into the light (Ephesians 5:11). Don't go into detail (Ephesians 5:12), but address the different edges of the coin of lust. Do this as a church and also in small groups, and be personally accountable (Hebrews 10:25). Think of lust as a *human* problem rather than a *personal* problem; it's all right to talk about it because it applies to everyone.

- Remember to pray about your online life.

- If looking at porn has been a particular problem, confess it – not just privately to God, but with a trusted person, perhaps with a church leader (James 5:16). Haul it out into the light (Ephesians 5:13–14). Lust is a sin like any other sin and worthy of no more, nor less, attention.

- Don't just focus on the negative sin. Increase your understanding of sex within marriage.

- Pray that God's spiritual fruit (and perhaps, especially, the fruit of self-control) will grow healthily within you (Galatians 5:22–23).

You were called to be free, so make a covenant with your eyes that you will not indulge them (Galatians 5:13). Instead, 'Stand firm, then, and do not let yourselves be burdened again by a yoke of slavery' (Galatians 5:1b). This is God's intention for you, and you are not alone; the Holy Spirit, and your Christian fellowship, are there to help you.

The biblical principle

I made a covenant with my eyes not to look lustfully.
JOB 31:1a

- Consider making a covenant with God about what you will and won't look at online. If it helps, make a contract; write it down and ask a trusted friend or two to witness it.

- Consider making a corporate covenant with a group of others, and build in accountability.

- Consider setting up 'parental controls' in your browser. You could ask a church leader to set the password (which you will never know and he or she will probably forget).

- Identify your temptation points and set up practical actions that will help you to 'flee'. If, for example, late-night browsing is a temptation point, disengage mid-evening and build a habit of doing something else before you go to sleep.

- Consider setting up an online 'buddy network' – where a trusted 'buddy' is notified if their tempted 'buddy' browses an inappropriate website.

Wisdom from the Psalms

I will sing of your love and justice;
    to you, Lord, I will sing praise.
I will be careful to lead a blameless life –
    when will you come to me?
I will conduct the affairs of my house
    with a blameless heart.
I will not look with approval
    on anything that is vile.
I hate what faithless people do;
    I will have no part in it.

PSALM 101:1–3

Some questions to think about

1 Preaching about porn in a Sunday service can stir up mixed opinions. Even though it affects all ages, it can be relegated to being a 'young people's' issue. Where, in your church, would it be appropriate and helpful to address it?

2 Lust is a human problem which, in some way, affects everyone. Who knows about your own, personal struggle with lust? If it is secret, why?

3 Do you pray before you browse? Do your children? If not, why not? Is there something practical you can do that will remind you to pray?

4

A personal digital pulpit

The way it is

The internet has turned human interaction upside down – literally. When Jesus taught, people gathered (offline) around him, because it was the only way to hear his words. This pattern of one person speaking to a listening crowd continued for almost 1,500 years and was extended with the invention of the printing press, which made it possible for one person (the author) to speak to a crowd (of readers) when they were not gathered physically in one place. In the 20th century, radio broadcasts and television extended the reach of speakers even further into individual homes, but it was still, essentially, the same pattern of one person speaking to a gathered crowd. The internet, however, has turned that traditional pattern on its head; now everyone in the crowd can post their opinion to the speaker.

This change may be for the better, or for the worse (and most people have an opinion… just look online!), but it's certainly different. Pre-internet lectures were only attended if they were helpful; music was released only if a recording company thought it would sell; books were published only if the publisher thought they were worth reading. In the internet age, anyone can post their lecture, music or novel regardless of whether anyone else is interested in it or not. There are pros and cons with both systems, and the new has not entirely replaced the old. In the Christian context, we still gather in offline crowds (in church) around preachers. In that sense, there has been no change in 2,000 years. The 'new system', though, is running concurrently with the old, and individuals in the congregation may be posting online while the preacher speaks. Everyone now has access to a digital pulpit.

Digging deeper

You may not wish to use the internet as a digital pulpit, and only use it for research, shopping and email. Fair enough. The moment you dip your toes into social media, though, or begin to blog, is the moment you stop having a choice. Whenever you venture an opinion, post or approve what someone else has posted, you are interacting with other people in the general 'marketplace' which is the internet (see Chapter 1). In this online arena, whatever you say, whether it is positive or negative, will be noted by someone and it becomes, whether you like it or not, a 'testimony'. Your interaction may testify to your holiness or to your lack of it – but it will testify.

Nearly 2,000 years ago, Paul said, 'We are therefore Christ's ambassadors, as though God were making his appeal through us' (2 Corinthians 5:20a). An ambassador represents their monarch or state and, while every ambassador has private downtime, their role is predominantly public. They are on show and those who meet them form an opinion of the monarch or state who sent them by what they see. This is what Paul had in mind when he calls himself an ambassador of Christ; he represents Christ and expects people to see Christ in him. With online interaction, welcome or not, Christians have an ambassadorial role which testifies to Christ, our monarch (or not), and others judge Christ by their interaction with us.

This ambassadorial role was alluded to in Chapter 2, where it was noted that what we post can either add weight to a Christian faith-view, or undo the work that God has already done in us. The bottom line is that unless Christians remember that the internet is, by its nature, a public place, we are likely to become ambassadors who mistake a public event for private downtime. Online interaction means that Christians are more on show than at any previous time in history.

Joining the dots

There's a difference between a soapbox and a pulpit. One is used for personal opinion, the other to open up the concerns of God. There are, of course, occasions when some preachers use their pulpit as a soapbox – and those who have gathered offline to listen are usually (rightly) unhappy about that. It's all too easy to find digital soapboxes online (sometimes it feels like there's nothing else), but digital pulpits come in various shapes and sizes. There are Christian blogs which are helpful, thought-provoking and edifying, which can be thought of as tall pulpits where the 'digital voice' reaches many people. A kind personal remark can be a pulpit too; it's a small one, but it doesn't need to be tall; it's a word of encouragement for just one person.

James says, 'My dear brothers and sisters, take note of this: everyone should be quick to listen, slow to speak and slow to become angry' (James 1:19). If that were an internet watchword, what a different arena it would be! But it isn't, and a great deal of online interaction is slow to listen, quick to speak and full of anger. If this makes you sad, you are in good company; whenever the actions of the human race bring us to tears, we are standing beside the Son of Man as he weeps (Luke 19:41–42) and acknowledging the work of the Holy Spirit in us as we share his grief.

Our ambassadorial status, however, is tested by what happens next – after we weep. When Jesus was grieved by human sin and faced significant opposition, he offered himself as the solution (1 Peter 2:22–24). Christians are called to do the same (1 Peter 2:20–21), and we should not expect this to be easy. Jesus says, 'Whoever wants to be my disciple must deny themselves and take up their cross daily and follow me' (Luke 9:23). A daily cross is, at the very least, significantly uncomfortable, and at worst, horribly painful. If we never receive an online crucifixion for posting what is right, our ambassadorial role probably means less than nothing, and it may mean that our online presence is actually counterproductive to Christianity – which we will look at in more detail in later chapters.

Pause for thought

Crowds are only ever a gathering of individuals, and God meets with individuals. The gate that leads to destruction is broad because people enter it in a crowd; the gate that leads to life is narrow because it is only one person wide (Matthew 7:13–14). The gate is Christ himself (John 10:9), and everyone goes through that gate alone (John 14:6). A crowd of thousands means nothing; what matters is whether anyone enters the gate. The size of the pulpit is irrelevant; what matters is that it signposts the gate.

A way forward

There's an old preacher's story about a Christian man (let's call him Fred), who believed that the proper way to testify to Christ was through his actions, not his words. So, he never spoke of his faith; instead, he tried to show honesty, kindness and generosity to everyone. A minister was speaking to another man about Christ and the man replied, 'I understand what you are saying. You say Christ changes people to become more godly, but I don't agree. There's a man I work with who's exactly as you describe and he's not a Christian. His name's Fred…'

Well, it's an old story and unlikely to be true, but it makes a point, and when it's applied to online interactions it's a helpful parable.

- If you say nothing from a faith viewpoint, others will assume you have no faith. Your digital pulpit then becomes a negative testimony.

- If you remark without joining what you remark to your faith, others will assume that's just your opinion. Your digital pulpit then becomes a missed opportunity.

- If you remark openly from a faith viewpoint, your use of your digital pulpit may be positive but unwelcome; it will depend on where in the online marketplace you have set it up (more on this in Chapter 6).

- If you take every opportunity to ram your online posts down everyone else's digital throat, they will avoid you, and you may also lose online friends who do not share your faith.

Ambassadorship may come automatically with new life in Christ, but it is a very particular life and role. Jesus said, 'By this everyone will know that you are my disciples, if you love one another' (John 13:35). Apply that to your online interactions and ask this question, 'Am I known by my love?' The answer will indicate whether your online life is an expression of your discipleship – or something else. Being known for standing on an online, digital soapbox is one thing, but if you are known for your love, you are probably occupying a digital pulpit even if you are unaware of it.

The biblical principle

> We are therefore Christ's ambassadors, as though God were making his appeal through us.
> 2 CORINTHIANS 5:20a

How can we apply this to our online lives?

- Keep praying before, during and after online interaction. Keep connected to the monarch you represent: Jesus Christ.

- Be quick to listen and slow to post (James 1:19), but post! Don't flee from the online marketplace; instead, consider what you can contribute – and contribute it.

- Consider the balance of your online social interaction. Some people react more than they initiate, while others initiate more than they react. If you are an ambassador for Christ, what does your monarch require of you?

- Consider adding a 'tagline' to your online profile which lets others know where you are coming from. For example, in 2017 (and it may have changed by now), my social media tagline read, 'I post mostly to amuse, sometimes to comment and discuss, but never to ridicule or abuse.' Not a specifically Christian tagline, but anyone who lands on my social media page sees that I am a vicar who writes Christian books so I didn't see the need to over-egg the pudding.

- Charles Sheldon wrote a novel in 1896 subtitled 'What would Jesus do?'[4] This tagline became very popular among late-20th-century Christians and many wore WWJD bracelets. Maybe a WWJP (What would Jesus post?) bracelet hovering above our keyboards might help ambassadors for Christ remember who they represent?

Wisdom from the Psalms

I will exalt you, my God the King;
    I will praise your name for ever and ever.
Every day I will praise you
    and extol your name for ever and ever.
Great is the Lord and most worthy of praise;
    his greatness no one can fathom.
One generation commends your works to another;
    they tell of your mighty acts.
They speak of the glorious splendour of your majesty –
    and I will meditate on your wonderful works.
They tell of the power of your awesome works –
    and I will proclaim your great deeds.

PSALM 145:1–6

Some questions to think about

1   Who is an ambassador for Christ – ministers, leaders, everyone? What makes a person an ambassador?

2   How do you currently occupy your personal digital pulpit? Is this under the direction of your monarch, or something that has just happened?

3   Consider some of your recent posts (and encourage your children to review theirs too), and ask: 'Is this something Jesus, or an ambassador of Christ, would post?'

5

Confessing an online past

The way it is

Over the last century, the United Kingdom, along with most of the developed and developing world, has experienced massive cultural and technological change. Social historians argue about the connections between cultural change and technological innovation, but within the remit of this book it's probably enough to recognise that the two are interconnected.

People who were born in the UK before the mid-1960s (the tech-immigrants) grew up in a society where the background cultural hum was Christianity, and in their formative years, they accessed the University of Life (through which they explored ideas outside of their formal education, and established their self-identity) through books, records, movies, radio and television. Each of these 'delivery methods' were extensions of the old system where one person spoke to a crowd – and individuals tended to identify with a group of others who 'gathered' around the same records, books, TV shows (and so forth). These groups (or 'tribes' as social historians might label them), usually numbered in the thousands or millions, and, therefore, self-identity tended to be expressed corporately and might well include a style of dress along with shared ideas and ideals.

People who have been born in the UK after the mid-1990s (the tech-indigenous) have grown up in a society where the background cultural hum has been 'individualism', and they have accessed the University of Life through the internet. Their taste in music, literature and entertainment may be utterly unique (they may be the *only* person who enjoys a particular artist; and that will probably be cherished because it means that they have fulfilled their cultural individualism exactly). Their understanding of religion and morality may also be similarly individualistic, and because the internet is their primary means of exploring ideas (with billions of remarks that purport to reflect normality but which probably reflect the opinion of only one person), they feel that they belong to a tribe of similarly minded people even though they are, in reality, quite alone. For the tech-indigenous, online interaction takes precedence over offline interaction – which is why they may ignore offline people around them while engaging online, text one another even when they are in the same building, or cluster around a phone screen.

It is against this background (of cultural individualism and online social interaction) that the rise of hook-up sex sites should be understood. It is natural for the tech-indigenous to look online for a sexual hook-up in the offline world. This tends to divorce sex from relationships, but this in itself is a facet of individualism, because it comes from a self-centred perspective.

Pause for thought

Self-centred is not the same as selfish. A selfish person fulfils their own needs at the expense of the needs of others. A self-centred person's starting point is their own needs, but they fulfil them by negotiation because they respect the self-centred starting point of others, and each interaction becomes a brief 'contract' of reciprocal, mutual, self-centred satisfaction.

Individualism is actually a new name for the oldest sin of all (theologians call it original sin), because it turns its back on dependence on God. In one sense, the technological portal through which individual sex is now pursued is simply a modern vehicle for another very old sin (promiscuity), but in another sense, online hook-up sites 'normalise' what Christianity defines as sin in a way that has never before been possible.

When a person in the tech-indigenous generation accepts new life through Christ and becomes a disciple, they confess their sin, turn from it and begin their new life as a new creation (2 Corinthians 5:17). They may need to apologise to those they have sinned against, seek their forgiveness and make amends (like Zacchaeus in Luke 19:8). They may need to rid themselves of artefacts which expressed their old life (like the Ephesian in Acts 19:18–19), and for some, that might include deleting past blogs and remarks which express opinions contrary to their new faith. The difficulty, though, is getting rid of their online sexual history. The sites used for hook-up sex may not allow individuals to delete previous content (including sexually explicit selfies), and what the new believer posted in the past may remain online as if it were current.

If you have not yet experienced this in your church, the key word is 'yet'.

Digging deeper

This issue (in the UK 21st-century church) is very similar to the first-century church's issue of needing to accommodate both Hebrew and Gentile believers whose backgrounds and attitudes were very different.

Those people who were born in the UK before the mid-1960s grew up against the background culture of Christianity, and may have been 'cultural Christians' (like my parents who, until they reached middle age, believed that because they were born in Britain, they were automatically Christian). People from this generation tended to retain Christian morality even when they turned their backs on religion. This meant that when churches engaged in evangelism in the 1960s and 1970s (although many didn't – they didn't see the need), they approached evangelism as, 'Christ adding a spiritual dimension' to an existing life which (in all but spiritual reality) was already being lived in an outwardly 'Christian fashion'. The focus of evangelism was, therefore, almost entirely 'internal' – it was about the personal relationship with Christ. In the 'old country' of the tech-immigrant generation, when someone came to faith, the way they lived their life often didn't need to change very much and, in this regard, they were similar to the Hebrew believers in the New Testament who, as Jews, already understood the laws of God and tried to live by them, and for whom the transition from Judaism to Christianity was 'linear'.

Those who have been born in the UK since the mid-1990s, however, have a cultural background more similar to the New Testament believers from Corinth or Ephesus. Those Gentile believers struggled to leave behind what had been normal in their pre-faith lives, which is why Paul addresses issues such as sexual immorality, impurity, greed and drunkenness (for example, Ephesians 5:3–21). When Gentiles became Christians, the new morality that came with their new life in Christ was far from 'linear'; it was a significant lifestyle 'step-change'. It is now much the same with many who have been born since the mid-1990s. Christian evangelism with the tech-indigenous generation is no longer only about an internal, spiritual challenge; it confronts lifestyle choices. It has to.

Within the first-century church, those who had come to a Christian faith out of Judaism were very anxious about those who had come to faith out of Gentile cultures. This led to a council in Jerusalem (Acts 15:1–35) where Paul spoke on behalf of the Gentile believers (Galatians 2:1–10), and some basic tenets of the Christian faith were established. The gulf between the two cultures, though, was vast – and not dissimilar to the current gulf between the UK tech-generations. How the gulf might be bridged is no mystery; it's the same now as it was then: 'There is neither Jew nor Gentile, neither slave nor free, nor is there male and female, for you are all one in Christ Jesus' (Galatians 3:28). Jesus is the bridge, whatever our background culture, opinions or baggage.

Pause for thought

When you read Paul's letters, notice that he mentions the sin of unbelievers but never criticises them for it; he only criticises Christian believers for sin. He expects God to judge everyone but says, in effect, 'Look what unbelievers do; well, they would do that because they don't know Christ; but you know Christ, so don't do it!' Instead of judging the actions of unbelievers, Paul invites unbelievers to judge the lives, actions and words of Christians – because he is confident that, as ambassadors for Christ, Christians demonstrate both the love of God and the transformational power of Christ. When Christians criticise unbelievers online for their sins, it's worth asking, 'Is that something Paul would post?'

Joining the dots

An individualistic culture thrives on celebrity and encourages everyone to aspire to fame. The internet offers the opportunity. Individualistic people measure their popularity and importance by the number of followers or friends their social media posts attract and, generally speaking, the more outrageous their online presence is, the more celebrity they accrue. Some vlog (video-blog) because they think their lives are of interest to others (and if they are right, advertising money will affirm their assumption with financial reward). This self-centred behaviour is applauded by an individualistic moral culture – but it can be very hard to leave behind when such a person finds faith. Potential employers search online as a matter of course; so do the 'self-righteous'; and so do mischief-makers. So, when someone leaves their 'old culture' behind to follow Christ, how do they do that when much of it remains online (having been approved and circulated by others and therefore having an ongoing 'life' beyond the originator's control)?

If you do not have anyone in your church who has come to Christ out of this culture (and needs help to start again), this is probably for one of two reasons. Either the people in your church (in this age group) are the children of existing church members (who grew up within the cultural 'walls' of your church) or this age-group is simply absent from your congregation. If they are missing, and you want to know where they are, they are online.

- If you don't have a church online presence – get one. That is where the tech-indigenous who are not in your church live.[5]

- Ensure that your online presence encourages those who land on your church website or social media page to think about Christ. Not just church – Christ.

A way forward

The church in the UK faces many challenges, but perhaps one of the biggest is allowing Christ to bridge the tech-generational divide between those who lead and form the majority of the congregation (the tech-immigrants… like me!) and the tech-indigenous who have never really heard about Christ at all. Like the Hebrew converts in the first-century church, it's all too common for the 21st-century tech-immigrants to sit happily in church listening to Bible readings about Jesus mixing with criminals, tax collectors and prostitutes, but for them to find it very hard to welcome the tech-indigenous generation who, like the Gentile converts in the first century, come from a culture where honesty, sexual integrity and spirituality have been entirely elastic.

The question which will define your church and establish whether it is ready to receive new believers is, 'How do we approach confession?' Paul was completely open about his past (1 Corinthians 15:9; Galatians 1:13–16a; Philippians 3:4b-6), and he was not alone (Acts 19:18). In our own time, before the internet arrived, personal sin could (and was) kept private; but now that the internet is with us, the past sin of new believers may be viewed by anyone who uses a search engine.

Any testimony to new life in Christ from the tech-immigrant generation tends to include vague allusions to past sins, but vague allusions sound (to the tech-indigenous), like, 'No sin here!' This gives rise to a mistaken belief that the tech-indigenous are somehow more sinful than the tech-immigrants ever were; which is, of course, a deception (1 John 1:8).

Confession is the only way to haul past lives into the light – especially if they are online and cannot be deleted. If they remain 'live', they must be admitted to and referred to as past. This can only be done in a church culture where those whose sins are 'hidden' in an offline past are *honest* about that past (and about their present struggles too), as Paul was. To put it bluntly, those who are new in the faith cannot be expected to set the tone of your church – they have only just arrived. The tone of your church must be set by its mature members. So, if your church wants the tech-indigenous to find and follow Christ, the tech-immigrants will have to get used to being honest about their offline sin (confessing), otherwise, those with an online sin-history will get the impression that *their* sins are, in comparison, 'like scarlet' (Isaiah 1:18), and they will avoid your church.

- Accept that most tech-indigenous people will arrive in your church with baggage that will horrify those who belong to the tech-immigrant generation. The pre-faith lives of this new 'Gentile generation' are going to look more like the life of a 1990s rock star than the 1960s bank-clerk pre-faith lives of the 'Hebrew generation'.

- Do what Paul did and address the issue with both generations. Work out where and how that can best be done in your church.

- Don't let anyone get away with ranking sin or comparing pasts. Sin is sin (Romans 3:9), confession is good (James 5:16) and what is past is past (Colossians 3:3).

- Figure out how to make confession honest without being salaciously detailed, and recognise that all sin is sinful; not just the 'eye-catching' stuff.

The biblical principle

If we confess our sins, he is faithful and just and will forgive us our sins and purify us from all unrighteousness.
1 JOHN 1:9

- How your church applies this principle to decades-old sin will determine how it is applied to recent online sin.

- How confession is regarded will set the tone.

Also, as something to consider, a new name can mark a new relationship with Christ. Simon became Peter (John 1:42); Joseph became Barnabas (Acts 4:36); Saul became Paul (Acts 13:9); and those who commit themselves to a monastic life accept a name change as a mark of their commitment. Christian baptism symbolises death to the old life and new birth in Christ (Romans 6:2–4) and in the UK, where elements of Christian culture remain in most national institutions, if anyone is baptised with a new name, that new name is accepted as a legal name change. In previous generations, when babies were commonly baptised, people carried their 'Christian names' from the beginning of their lives. These days, when fewer babies are baptised and the adult baptism of new believers is more common, a name change at baptism can be a powerful statement. Their old life and name is dead in Christ, and they begin a new life of freedom in Christ with a new name (John 8:36).

Wisdom from the Psalms

Have mercy on me, O God,
    according to your unfailing love;
according to your great compassion
    blot out my transgressions.
Wash away all my iniquity
    and cleanse me from my sin.
For I know my transgressions,
    and my sin is always before me.
PSALM 51:1–3

Some questions to think about

1 How can your church help young people to stop building an inappropriate online presence before they start? How can it best do this?

2 How does your church help parents (to help their children) understand that future difficulties can be avoided by recognising the public (and possibly permanent) nature of the internet?

3 Does your church encourage a culture of open, honest confession from everyone?

6

Sowing digital seed

The way it is

Some Christians will want their online life to be overtly evangelistic, some will run screaming from the idea and most will hope that they will, from time to time, post something of spiritual value. Working on the assumption that those who are not interested in connecting their faith with their online life will not be reading this book, I'll assume that every reader is, to some extent, interested, and hopes that they will be able to sow some 'digital seed'.

'Seed sowing' is an interesting concept, and it's worth considering what it means in the offline world. Most churches and Christians are familiar with the term. When a church event (or personal conversation about faith) has taken place and there has been no visible sign of a response, someone may well say, 'Well, at least a seed was sown.' In one sense, this is absolutely right because the intention of the event or conversation was to share something of Christ and, if nothing else, a seed probably was sown. In another sense, though, it is absolutely wrong because sowing is not a stand-alone process.

Think of it this way. You buy a packet of flower seeds, go out into your garden and scatter them (sow them) on your lawn. Why would you do that? The chances of any of those seeds germinating is remote and, even if one or two make it, the next time you mow your lawn you will kill them. Why would you take comfort in telling yourself, 'Well, at least a seed was sown'? Most people would look at the back of the seed packet, prepare the soil (or a pot in their greenhouse) and sow the seeds according to the instructions.

Sowing is part of a process. If you sow in a lawn, or in a bramble patch, or on concrete, you are wasting your effort and, even when a seed is sown in appropriate soil, it needs further tending if the plant is to grow. Paul understood this: 'I planted the seed, Apollos watered it, but God has been making it grow' (1 Corinthians 3:6); and we should understand this too. Sowing seed any-old-where is a result of not understanding the need to find the right kind of soil in which to sow.

Throughout, however, it's important to remember that the point of sowing is not to sow but, as Jesus says in his parable, for the seed to grow and produce a multiplicity of what was sown (Mark 4:20). In other words, the act of sowing is the first step; the seed growing (in a person's life) is the second; the seed being re-sown (by that person) is the third. The spiritual harvest is therefore not judged by the number of seeds sown, or even by the number of people who respond to the initial sowing; it is judged by the number of people who themselves become sowers.

Digging deeper

Jesus' parable of the sower (Mark 4:3–9; which he explains in vv. 10–20) says that a farmer sows the seed – which locates the act of sowing in an agricultural field which, as Jesus' listeners will have known, had already been prepared (probably by ploughing). There is no suggestion that the farmer sowed his seed in the marketplace, on a dockside or up a mountain; the farmer sowed his seed in a field. Even then, some of the seed fell on the path, some on rocky patches and some amongst thorns (presumably at the edge of the field). Even though this was a prepared field, some of the seed was lost, but other seed fell on good soil and produced a harvest. The focus of the parable is not the seed but the soil; it's the same seed, and whether it grows depends on the soil, not the seed.

Think of the soil in terms of Matthew 10:5–14 where Jesus sends his disciples out to preach (v. 7). They are sent out to sow the seed of the kingdom and they are instructed to find suitable 'soil'. If the soil is good, they are to stay and sow (vv. 11–13); if the soil is rocky, they are to move on (v. 14). Jesus' instructions indicate that there is no point sowing the seed of the kingdom in soil where it will not grow.

This pattern (of seeking out suitable soil) seems to be how Paul and the other apostles operated when they arrived in a new town. Most of the time they headed straight for the synagogue – for the people who already believed in the God of Judaism (for example, Acts 13:5; 13:14; 14:1 and so forth). They also found the places where those who 'believed in God' (Gentiles who accepted the God of Judaism as the one true God) gathered for prayer (for example, Acts 16:13). Although it's common to hear preachers today declare that 'Paul preached in the marketplace', he doesn't seem to have done this in the book of Acts. Why would he? Seed scattered in the marketplace would be trampled underfoot! It's true that Paul took every opportunity to sow the seed of the kingdom and was happy to use any venue, such as the place of debate in Athens (Acts 17:22) or the lecture hall of Tyrannus in Ephesus (Acts 19:8–9), but he never 'broadcast the seed' in soil where there was no hope of growth. He headed for soil that had already been prepared; he went to where people were already thinking about God.

Pause for thought

Seeds can grow anywhere – trees on chimney stacks, flowers in cracked asphalt – but these are the exceptions. Most seeds grow in prepared ground. If Christians do not seek out prepared ground, and rely solely on exceptional seeds, the church will decline.

Joining the dots

Focusing on sowing 'digital seed' online, let's consider Jesus' parable of the sower:

- **Seed on the path**. The soil on the path is compacted by footfall and seed on the path will be trampled; it's the equivalent of sowing seed on a pavement. Online, social media is fast-moving with quick responses and little reflection. With the exception of closed social media groups, open social media sites can be thought of as 'online paths' where the volume and speed of digital traffic makes the ground very hard – and online 'birds' are always circling, just waiting to peck away at anything they disagree with.

- **Seed on rocky patches**. Here the soil is shallow, and while seed appears to grow, there is no depth and the sun scorches it to nothing. These are the interminably pedantic arguments which some people engage in because it entertains them to argue. Such arguments may be about science versus religion, or how a God of love can allow suffering, but they lead nowhere, the arguments become vitriolic and people back off and disappear. If online conversations lead to shouty outcomes, it's probably a sign that they have no spiritual depth.

- **Seed amongst thorns**. These can be thought of as conversations with those who are on the edge of faith but cannot commit to Christ because of lifestyle choices which choke the spiritual seed (about money, sexual relationships, and so forth). Online, this tends to describe individuals who want Christians to tell them that their lifestyle is fine – even when it conflicts with Christian values.

- **The good soil**. This soil produces a faith-harvest of people who themselves become seed-sowers – offline and online.

A way forward

Paul and the apostles headed for the synagogues, the places of prayer and the arenas for open discussion. The online equivalents are interest-based forums, chat rooms and feedback groups. If you want to sow digital seed, then head for where the soil is appropriate:

- In the offline world, Christians might learn a language, join a painting group or a sports team because they are interested in that activity; but they may also hope to make new friends and have an opportunity to 'sow seed'. Online, it's much the same – head for a forum that interests you; get to know the other people and let them get to know you.

- Continue to pray about your online life, and pray for the people you interact with. In a forum setting, it might then be appropriate (from time to time) to offer to pray offline for expressed needs – as you might do for someone in your offline drama group or football team.

- Recognise that any plant that grows as a result of your digital sowing will need to be rooted in the offline world. If the person concerned lives at a distance to you (perhaps even on another continent), you will need to encourage them to connect with their local church (not yours). This means that sowing digital seed will probably not increase the size of your church – but it may increase the number of people in God's kingdom.

- Take a long look at your church's website and/or social media page. These are, primarily, online billboards (platforms for information about service times and so forth, and where you advertise, with pictures, your latest successful event). This means that most people will filter out 'spiritual content' because it's generally not what they are looking for, so you are unlikely to sow digital seeds through your billboards; but you may be able to direct people who land on your site (or page) to a discussion forum full of seed. One idea might be to develop a 'Christianity FAQ' page with a linked discussion forum.

The biblical principle

> Do not be deceived: God cannot be mocked. People reap what they sow. Whoever sows to please their flesh, from the flesh will reap destruction; whoever sows to please the Spirit, from the Spirit will reap eternal life.
> GALATIANS 6:7–8

The basic challenge is: what are you hoping to 'sow' online?

- If Christians 'sow' entirely about themselves (in other words, use the internet for self-promotion) that is 'sowing to the flesh' and they will reap what they sow. It's worth, from time to time, taking stock of your online life to reflect on what you are sowing, where and why.

- If you sow simply to make your church 'bigger', that is sowing in the flesh too. It's no coincidence that churches which take pride in their size grow… and then fail.

- Sowing digital seed is spiritually intentional. Although it is 'online', it is still personal, and its aim is for individuals to reap eternal life, grow in faith and to become sowers themselves.

- Because sowing (both offline and online) is personal, it requires a level of sacrifice. Expect a percentage of 'young shoots' to fail. Be ready to point people to God and to another church (rather than to yours). Be ready for grief as well as joy. In other words, follow Christ.

Wisdom from the Psalms

Those who sow in tears
　　will reap with songs of joy.
Those who go out weeping,
　　carrying seed to sow,
will return with songs of joy,
　　carrying sheaves with them.

PSALM 126:5–6

Some questions to think about

1　How intentional are you about sowing digital seed? Where do you currently sow it? Are you sowing in the right places?

2　How much online time are you prepared to spend with people who show no signs of any seed growing? What are your exit strategies?

3　How much online time are you prepared to spend with people who (because of where they live) will never join your church?

7

Stewards of a digital tongue

The way it is

The internet, as everyone knows, can be a shouty, rude environment. Criminal activity and behaviour are dealt with by the police, and personal abuse can be reported to ISPs and websites, but this still leaves a background hum of ill-mannered unpleasantness. Many internet users find themselves wondering, 'Why doesn't someone do something about it?'

The answer to that question is in the American Telecommunications Act 1996, which President Clinton declared (when he signed it) would 'civilise the Wild West of the internet'. Generally speaking, it did, but in this legislation, under Clause 230 ('Treatment of Publisher or Speaker'), it states that neither the 'provider' nor the 'interactive user' is the 'publisher or speaker' of content posted by someone else. In other words, whereas an offline book publisher can be taken to court along with an author whose offensive work they published, a website cannot (and neither can you, as an 'interactive user', by dint of something someone else has posted on your webpage, unless you condone it). The next declaration under Clause 230 ('Civil Liability') allows websites and interactive users to remove content posted by someone else according to their own subjective decision. It is this Telecommunications Act that makes the (mostly American-based) websites what they are, and explains why 'no one does anything about' online unpleasantness – it's not, legally, the website's problem, and they can make their own choices about what is removed and what remains.

In the developed world, where citizens are used to protective legislation in almost every area of offline life, the online onslaught can come as something of a shock because, in the offline world, people cannot get away with it. In reality, though, this means that online interaction is similar to the offline life experienced by the apostles who had little legal protection and, even when the law *was* applied, it was applied subjectively by whoever was in charge (for example, at the trial of Jesus, when Pilate pretty much made it up as he went along). This makes the New Testament applicable to online behaviour from an identical standpoint; while it is not possible to alter the way *others* speak, Christians have an obligation to steward *their own* speech.

Digging deeper

Jesus, James, Paul and Peter all warn how quickly the tongue can lead both the speaker and listener astray. Jesus speaks of words making the speaker 'unclean' (Matthew 15:11). Paul contrasts unwholesome words with words that build up and benefit those who hear them, and implies that unwholesome words grieve the Holy Spirit (Ephesians 4:29–30). Peter exhorts Christians to keep their tongues from evil, to resist repaying insult with insult and to return, instead, a blessing (1 Peter 3:9–10), and in this he is almost directly quoting Jesus (Luke 6:28). James, however, has the most to say about the tongue.

James likens the tongue to the bit in a horse's mouth, the rudder that steers a ship and the spark that begins a forest fire (James 3:3–5). He goes on to say that the tongue can corrupt a person entirely (v. 6) and describes it as untameable, restless for evil and full of poison. James, for one, would not have been remotely surprised by what is posted online! His focus, though, is not the whole human race, but Christian people. Are Christians part of the background roar? James admits that, all too often, they are, but should not be (vv. 9–12), and goes on to say that they must submit all that they are (including their tongues and wrongly motivated actions), to God (James 4:7–10).

Paul tells Titus to 'remind the people... to slander no one, to be peaceable and considerate, and always to be gentle toward everyone' (Titus 3:1–2). That may not be the intention of many who go online, but it can be the intention of Christians.

Joining the dots

'Double-minded' Christians (James 4:8) have always been a source of concern. Historically, the 'double-minded' have been the people (who exist in most congregations) who worship on Sunday and say all the 'right things' in small groups but who, in private 'round-the-back' conversations, eviscerate others with their remarks. They are the people out of whose mouths come both praise to God and curses to people (James 3:9–10). In the past, these verbal assassinations tended to be whispered in private; these days they appear online. When this happens, this gives substance to the old criticism that 'Christians are hypocrites; they say one thing in church and the opposite everywhere else', and the online remarks of the few can destroy the credibility of the many. This kind of online vitriol therefore needs to be challenged by church leaders – and the person concerned encouraged to 'come near to God' and purify their double mindedness (James 4:8). Everyone else, however, also needs to be careful; after all, 'We all stumble in many ways' (James 3:2), and our own digital tongue is only ever one knee-jerk post from sparking a new forest fire (v. 5b). The key to stewarding the digital tongue is:

- Remember that the internet is a public forum. Keep in mind the person you would least wish to read what you are about to post, and recognise that this person will probably read it.

- Remember that you are an ambassador for Christ; people will judge Christ by your words.

Pause for thought

'A soothing tongue is a tree of life, but a perverse tongue crushes the spirit' (Proverbs 15:4). Does your digital tongue crush the spirit or encourage life?

The 'spark that starts the fire' is, however, only one aspect of the digital tongue and tends to apply to social media. There are others.

In the offline world, words contribute only a small percentage of what is said. Inflection, pauses and body language all speak volumes and can communicate more than the words themselves. The online world, however, is text-dependent, and while emojis attempt to indicate emotions, that is all they do – indicate. This text-dependency impacts any relationship that begins online. Skype (and similar websites) allows people to see and hear the other person, and those who message people they already know in the offline world are extending an existing relationship, but those who *begin* a relationship through text-based messages can easily go astray. If they are not careful, the person receiving the message adds imagined intonation and non-verbal communication into the words they are reading; the person they are corresponding with does the same thing, and the whole relationship develops as a kind of interactive fiction where both correspondents shape the other into someone they are not. Leaving aside those who deceive to groom, this is what happens when people genuinely fall in love online but, when they meet offline, discover that their beloved is not as they imagined. The key word is: 'imagined'.

Stewarding our digital tongue applies to any online arena which is typescript based. It includes sending texts and emails that were intended to be straightforward but cause offence to others; receiving correspondence which we ourselves find offensive (where the intention was probably anything but); and generally leaping to conclusions. Stewarding our digital tongue includes considering who we are corresponding with, and taking care over the words we choose when messaging someone we do not know in the offline world.

Another aspect of stewarding our digital tongue is our mindset when we blog or offer a considered view. In 1985, I attended a Communications Course in the Diocese of Oxford where it was suggested that before speaking or writing, three questions should be asked (in order):

1 What do I expect 'the crowd', or the individual, to do about what I'm about to communicate? How do I want them to respond? The answer could be, 'I just want them to know this,' or, 'I want them to pray about this,' or, 'I want them to respond in the following practical way...' and so forth. The important thing, though, is to know how you expect them to respond.

2 Who am I communicating with?

3 What shall I say?

This struck me at the time as incredibly important, and it has stuck with me. For example, in the offline world, we have probably all heard sermons where there was a sense of gathering excitement and expectation, only for the preacher to finish and sit down... and the sense of something impending to fizzle away. When that happens, the preacher, when preparing their sermon, probably only asked question three (what shall I say?). When they preached, they, too, probably had a sense of something important happening, but no idea what anyone should do about it (question one). Similarly, we have probably all been present when someone delivered a children's talk to pensioners or a theological treatise to infants (who never thought about question two). And... let's acknowledge the whole area of offline notice boards, magazines and news sheets which are not the subject of this book.[6]

In the online world, before you blog or post a considered view, avoid the temptation to only ask, 'What should I say?' Try asking the three questions in order, because what you should say is, in fact, the least important question. If you know how you want people to respond, and have considered who you are talking to, what you should say will be obvious – and if you prayerfully ask these questions before God, you will be stewarding your digital tongue for the benefit of others (Ephesians 4:29).

A way forward

The internet can feel like a lumbering, destructive behemoth, but one small rudder can change the direction of a massive container ship. The Christian tongue can be that rudder in our online interactions (James 3:4). Paul says, 'Let your conversation be always full of grace, seasoned with salt, so that you may know how to answer everyone' (Colossians 4:6). Given that much internet conversation is full of salt and seasoned with very little grace, how refreshing it is to offer an alternative! None of us, individually, can change the direction of the entire web, but we can each connect with our own online network, full of grace and seasoned with salt:

- Be generous and sprinkle salty truth sparingly, and it will give your online words flavour. Dump salty truth online with little grace and anyone with an open wound will run screaming in pain.

- Remember: online interaction is not 'down-time' from your faith. You are an ambassador for Christ and you are on show.

The biblical principle

> The heart of the righteous weighs its answers,
>   but the mouth of the wicked gushes evil.
> PROVERBS 15:28

- Be intentional about your online contribution and take your time. When engaging on social media, think before responding; your remark may benefit from waiting five minutes.

• Your online words indicate your heart. If you are double-minded about Christ, your online life will reveal it. You can't steward your digital tongue if your heart is pulling in two different directions.

Wisdom from the Psalms

I will extol the Lord at all times;
    his praise will always be on my lips.
I will glory in the Lord;
    let the afflicted hear and rejoice.
Glorify the Lord with me;
    let us exalt his name together.
PSALM 34:1–3

Some questions to think about

1 When your church teaches about Christian behaviour, does it include teaching about your online life? Does it spell out the importance of what should not be posted, alongside what should?

2 Are you double-minded about Christ? What is at the root of your double-mindedness? Where will you confess this, and who will help you in your discipleship?

3 Think about the different online 'arenas' where you interact with others; what kind of stewardship of your digital tongue is appropriate for each arena?

8

Always in the presence of God

The way it is

Christian 'double-mindedness' is often revealed by speech (see Chapter 7) but it shows up in many areas of life. Trusting God but relying on money is one example, because there is a tension between praying in the Lord's Prayer, 'Give us today our daily bread' (Matthew 6:11), and the fact that our homes are full of stored food and we have money in the bank for the next supermarket shop. On a more insidious level, tithing (setting aside a percentage of income for charities) can also lead to double-mindedness. It's not uncommon for Christians to slip into thinking that their money tithe is 'God's bit' while the rest of their income is theirs to spend as they please. The Bible, however, makes it clear (from Genesis 1—2, through Psalm 24:1 to Hebrews 2:10) that human beings are only stewards of the creation, and that everything in it continues to belong to God. In other words, there is no 'God's bit' or 'our bit' in any area of life; it all belongs to God. Our attitude to money is an area which, like a litmus test, indicates whether we are single-minded or double-minded about God (as Jesus made clear in Matthew 6:24).

Money is not the subject of this book, but those who slip into this kind of 'sectional' attitude towards money easily slip into similar attitudes about time and activity. Once a person thinks about money in terms of 'God's bit' and 'my bit', it's a short step into thinking about their life in the same way. When this happens, church attendance, church work, personal prayer (and so forth) are thought of as 'God's bit'; work, school and chores are thought of as 'neutral bits that just have to happen'; and leisure time and activities quickly become thought of as 'my bit'. This kind of double-mindedness (or even triple-mindedness) tends to show up in one (or all) of the following ways:

- The person's offline tongue indicates their double-mindedness. They proclaim themselves to be Christian, but in private conversations they embrace very different attitudes and standards.

- Because online interaction gives the illusion of privacy (see Chapter 1), the double-minded person's online activity tends to indicate their true heart. This may be exposed when a pillar of the church is revealed to have a porn addiction, but it may equally show up as an inability to deal with online difficulty or challenge with grace. When they are caught out by a remark they have posted in haste, or receive an unjust criticism, the double-minded tend to retaliate hard and fast, intending to hurt and maim.

As we established in Chapter 1, what is whispered in the online ear tends to be shouted from the digital rooftops, so our online life will indicate to others (and ourselves, if we will listen) where we are with God. If we are single-minded believers, it will show; if we are double-minded, that will show too; and the difference is about whether we live our lives in active recognition that we are always in the presence of God.

Digging deeper

The old covenant expressed the relationship between God and his people: 'I will take you as my own people, and I will be your God' (Exodus 6:7a). As with any covenant, there were two sides. God covenanted to oversee the nation of Israel and, through them, to bring all nations under his loving rule. They covenanted to worship God and keep his laws (which, as the ten commandments made clear, applied to every aspect of life whether it was religious, secular or private). The understanding was that, although temple worship was located in Jerusalem, in daily life, regardless of where they were or what they were doing, they were always in the presence of God (Psalm 139:7).

The new covenant fulfils the intention of the old covenant in the person of Jesus. He became Immanuel, 'God with us' (Matthew 1:23), and he fulfilled the old covenant (Matthew 5:17) by becoming the mediator of the new covenant (Hebrews 8:6–13), which was sealed by the Holy Spirit (Ephesians 1:13–14) on and after Pentecost (Acts 2:32–33). The promise of the old covenant is now fulfilled in the new as, through Jesus Christ, it becomes possible for people from all nations to become God's own people (Matthew 28:18–20). Christians, therefore, confirm that, 'God is their God and they are his people,' and it is still a two-sided covenant. God covenants new life to human beings through the self-giving sacrifice of Christ (John 3:16–18a); in response, believers covenant their lives to God in Christ as a living sacrifice (Romans 12:1); and the Holy Spirit brings new life and makes obedience to God's law possible (Romans 7:6).

Christians acknowledge that we are always in the presence of God. When we are in church worshipping, we are in his presence. When we are at home watching television, we are in his presence too. It makes no difference whether we are in the bath, at the supermarket, with others, on our own, awake or asleep – we are in his presence. And when we are online, we are in his presence too. If we are in any measure double-minded about Christ, we will 'partition' his presence, and behave as if he is absent from certain parts of our lives. The truth is, though, that even if we think there are areas of life where we can somehow 'shut him out', we are always in his presence, whether we are aware of it or not.

No one is without sin. Even the holiest people sin regularly, and everyone is a work in progress (1 John 1:8–9; Philippians 3:12). However, whereas the double-minded person wants God in a *bit* of their life, the single-minded person wants God in *all* of their life;

full stop (Philippians 3:13–14); no matter how far short they still fall. Ironically, what often distinguishes the double-minded from the single-minded is that, while the double-minded are satisfied with their discipleship, the single-minded, like Paul, are not. The single-minded are all too aware of their own shortcomings, and understand that the solution is in Christ (Romans 7:14–25).

Pause for thought

Double-minded Christians, although satisfied with themselves, tend to be restless with others. In the offline world, they 'church-hop' (attend a church for a while, become dissatisfied and move on to another church). They know they are not connecting with God but they think the church they are attending is the problem. As well as church-hopping in the offline world, they preacher-hop online too, and rarely apply anything they hear into offline action. The problem (and the solution) is not located in a particular church or online, but in the person's own heart – 'You will seek me and find me when you seek me with all your heart' (Jeremiah 29:13).

Joining the dots

When you are online, you are in the presence of God. Whether you are playing an online game, catching up with friends, engaging in debate, doing research, expressing an opinion, visiting a 3D vista or just having fun – you are in the presence of God. It's a fact of (created) life, and new technology is neither 'higher' nor 'deeper' than the Spirit of God. You are 'there' and he is 'there' too (Psalm 139:8–10).

- When you are online, you are in the presence of God; do you know what God wants of you (John 14:26)? Have you asked?
- Remember: you are in the presence of God; don't put out the Spirit's fire by what you post or where you visit (1 Thessalonians 5:19).
- And don't panic; pray (Philippians 4:6–7)!

A way forward

Your single-minded or double-minded faith is unlikely to be revealed in situations when you know you are on public show, or when you are in control of events, or when you are with people who like you and agree with you (more on this in Chapter 17). These are not testing situations. The test comes when you feel you are entirely alone, or when unpleasant things take you by surprise, or when you are with people who don't like you or agree with you. You can avoid being tested in the offline world by avoiding any area or people who might create difficulty, but avoiding being tested online is much harder. You are only ever one click away from an opinion, or a person, you would never interact with in the offline world.

- Accept that any double-mindedness in you will be exposed. If (or when) it is, accept that too. Ask the Spirit of God to change you, and make his forgiveness and grace part of your current, honest 'confession' (see Chapter 5).

- If you are tempted to visit websites you know you should not visit, accept that there is double-mindedness in you. If you want Christ, give this temptation over to God in a similar manner to sexual temptations (see Chapter 3).

- If you are aware of other church members being double-minded online, help them (Galatians 6:1). Approach them privately; if they will not even listen, include others (Matthew 18:15–17).

The biblical principle

'For in him we live and move and have our being.' As even some of your own poets have said, 'We are his offspring.'
ACTS 17:28

We are all God's 'offspring' (children) and children make mistakes. Be quick to listen, slow to speak and slow to anger (James 1:19); because you are only ever one click away from slipping up yourself!

Wisdom from the Psalms

Where can I go from your Spirit?
    Where can I flee from your presence?
If I go up to heaven, you are there;
    if I make my bed in the depths, you are there.
If I rise on the wings of the dawn,
    if I settle on the far side of the sea,
even there your hand will guide me,
    your right hand will hold me fast.
PSALM 139:7–10

Some questions to think about

1 Does knowing that you are always in the presence of God embarrass you in any way? Is there an area of your offline life you would prefer to be private from God? How about your online life?

2 Most people have a particular weakness which makes them slip into double-mindedness; what is yours? Who knows about it (and they only need to know the general gist, not necessarily the details)? In what practical ways are you addressing this?

3 Are your online posts and remarks consistent with someone who proclaims Christ? (In other words, do they indicate a single-minded faith?)

9

Wisdom and discernment

The way it is

A distressing news item appears in your social media feed: 'Rubovian Christians forced to flee homes by atheist regime!' You click through to an online article and you are appalled; the way these Rubovian Christians are being treated is sickening! You note that this news item has already been circulated three million times so you circulate it too – you want your friends to know. You also sign a parliamentary petition demanding that the treatment of Rubovian Christians be debated in the House of Commons and email the link to your church leader and ask what your church is doing about the situation… and you have just added your weight to an item of fake news! I know it's fake because I, David Robertson, have just made it up, and if you have any remaining doubts, Rubovia was a fictional country invented by Gordon Murray for a children's puppet show (aired by the BBC in the 1950s), in which one of the more memorable characters was a baby dragon called Pongo who turned into a cabbage when he sneezed![7]

Unhappily, fake news items are a reality and so are 'alternative facts' (as they have been coined in some political circles). Both are clever; they look and sound factual, and they are designed to deceive. If you have never been taken in, you are doing better than most, and Christians, in particular, can be easily deceived; because Christians tend to be honest, they expect honesty from others.

Professional-looking websites are part of the problem. Anyone who knows their way around a computer can set up a fantastic website, and those visiting the site will not be able to tell if it represents a multinational organisation with millions of supporters... or one person sitting in their bedroom propounding a philosophy that only they believe. The real problem, though, is a fundamental misunderstanding about what the internet actually is.

The internet is primarily a marketplace where most websites are shop windows. Your church website or social media page is a kind of shop window too; it's where people in the 'online high street' can peer in and decide if they want to visit. Your online shop is not selling a product (unless your church knits hats and sells them through your website) but it is 'selling' your church. Other websites are just shops that sell books, music, household items, car parts... anything and everything; others sell political and religious ideals; others sell their particular altruistic concerns (such as conservation issues); but the vast majority of websites are 'selling' something. The key question is, how do these 'online shops', in such a crowded online marketplace, attract customers?

At the malignant end of the internet, the answer is: by frightening people. The intention of fake news is then to paint nightmare scenarios so that those who are posting it can claim that only *they* can deliver everyone from the coming Armageddon.[8] These kind of posts tend to be politically, racially, ideologically or religiously motivated, and usually emanate from hard-line beliefs.

At the benign end of the internet, posts about cats, quizzes, funny fake news or 'alternative facts' are posted by businesses or individuals seeking to improve their profile on social media and their ranking on search engines. They do this by posting content that will be circulated millions of times (they hope), because every time their post is circulated (by you and others), their business (or personal interest) rises up the search-visibility rankings. The business or individual who posted the video (or quiz, etc.) probably has no interest in the content itself; all they want is for you to circulate it, increase their overall online visibility, and make it more likely that the 'customers' in whom they are *really* interested will find *their* online 'shop' when they browse for a product (or for their political or religious ideal), and 'buy' it from them.

Digging deeper

Jesus said, 'Be as shrewd as snakes and as innocent as doves' (Matthew 10:16b). He said this because he was aware that he was sending his disciples into a world full of fallen people; he was 'sending them out like sheep among wolves' (Matthew 10:16a). In the offline world, we are all aware of this and pick up from non-verbal communication when someone is not being straight with us. There are also places we would not visit without a police escort, and most people adjust their behaviour depending on the time of day – for example, there are places where we would happily walk alone in daylight but would never venture into after dark. Online, though, the only visual clues are the pixels on our screen; we are sitting at home or on a train in safety, and it is very hard to tell 'where we are'. Jesus' instruction, then, is highly pertinent. As a Christian, approach every website, blog and post as a benign lamb – but don't be deceived; the person communicating with you may have wolfish intent.

This theme of caution is continued by Jesus in his teaching about prophets and teachers. He warns that some will be false, so don't just listen to what they say, look at the way they live, because this will indicate their real agenda (Matthew 7:15–20; 23:1–39). Online, it's not possible to see how people live, but it is possible to search out their other posts and activities and to form an opinion about where they are coming from, and why.

Paul also cautions Christians against false teachers and puts some of the blame on those who so readily listen. He says that, 'to suit their own desires, they will gather around them a great number of teachers to say what their itching ears want to hear' (2 Timothy 4:3b). In our own day, that prophecy is clearly accurate; the internet is full of self-styled teachers ready to scratch 'itchy ears'!

Peter, too, cautions against 'cleverly devised stories' and false teachers (2 Peter 1:16; 2:1–22). In fact, the general opinion seems to be that Christian believers should test out *everything* they hear, even when it comes from the mouths of their own leaders (2 Peter 2:1; Romans 16:17–18; Galatians 1:6–8).

The New Testament message is clear; followers of the Lamb of God (John 1:29) belong to his flock – but there are wolves out there… so be snaky-shrewd!

Joining the dots

Be aware that while television and magazines (broadcast and published media) are governed by advertising standards, much of the internet is not (because, according to the American Telecommunications Act 1996, websites are not broadcasters or publishers). The big websites are shops, and although they may appear 'free to use', the 'terms and conditions' you sign in order to access them allows them to 'mine' your personal details (more on this in Chapter 16).

The holy grail of advertising is *targeted advertising*. Computers are good at handling data and, every time you log on and search, or browse and buy, or approve and circulate, or blog and discuss, the website you are using takes note (whether the website is a search engine, a social media platform, a shop or an email account). This means that adverts can be tailored, pretty much, just to you. This is why, when you browse (or mention) a product on one website, adverts for similar products pop up on other websites you are using. This is done routinely and, if it frustrates you, it happens because you agreed to it when you clicked 'I agree to the terms and conditions' of that website. It's also why you are allowed to use that website for 'free'. Every time you click on an ad, even when you don't buy the product, the business that put it there pays the website. The internet is a marketplace; expect ads.

This kind of tailored advertising is also increasingly used by politicians. Use a search engine to browse 'Project Alamo' and you will discover how, in 2017, a company called Cambridge Analytica managed the social media campaign of one of the American presidential candidates. Using an 85-million-dollar budget, social media ads were targeted at the American voting public at a rate of 35 to 40 *thousand* variations *per day* until they were refined by how individuals reacted to them. Voters then received ads that made absolute sense to *them*, and this kind of advertising is entirely legal; after all, everyone clicked that little 'I agree to the terms and conditions' button.

In this regard, the internet is more like the first-century world of the apostles than the offline 21st-century world we also inhabit. There were no advertising standards back then and it is not dissimilar online. So, take Jesus' advice; be as innocent as doves and as shrewd as serpents!

Pause for thought

What was the last thing that caught your eye on social media, which you then circulated? Did you research it in any way to test out whether it was benign or malignant before you circulated it? Did you even note the company or individual who initiated it (there will be a link below the post)?

A way forward

Remember… every time you go online, you are entering a marketplace. In the offline world, you ignore ads on TV and on high-street hoardings, so why would you accept online ads as gospel truth? Also remember that, while offline ads are required to be truthful, this is not necessarily applied online (they can be similar to the offline ads of the 1950s which, for example, promoted alcohol and cigarettes as part of a healthy, sophisticated lifestyle), and you may not even be aware that something that has caught your interest is even an ad!

- Understand that you are not using the internet for free. Watch out, especially, for political, ideological and religious ads. Your reaction may be the innocent, interested 'bleat' of a lamb, but the advertiser may be disguising its wolfish 'teeth'.

- If your ears are itchy, get them scratched in your local church. If your local church doesn't scratch where you are itching, it could be the fault of the church… or a fault in you (see Chapter 8). Watch out for your own spiritual double-mindedness.

- Get used to discerning the truth even in your local church. Be an active listener and test out what you hear. Preachers will welcome this; their interest is the kingdom of God, not their own glory (unless they are false teachers, that is).

- Test everything you read and see online. Is it what it purports to be? Before you circulate it, check it out; who initiated it?

- Understand 'clickbait' – the funny videos, the intriguing pieces of news, the salacious gossip, the harmless quizzes, the flattering quizzes (nine out of ten people can't answer this), and so on and so forth. They are all there to entice you to click on them. When you click, someone, somewhere, mines your details and knows that little bit more about you – which makes it even more likely that you will receive the kind of clickbait that *you* are likely to respond to.

The biblical principle

I am sending you out like sheep among wolves. Therefore, be as shrewd as snakes and as innocent as doves. Be on your guard.
MATTHEW 10:16–17a

- Read the temptation of Jesus (Matthew 4:1–11) and think of it as a wolf-attack on the Lamb of God. Ask yourself, have *you* ever been tempted to try and turn rocks into bread? Probably not… because you are not Jesus. What tempts *you* is always tailored personally to you, just as it was to Jesus; that's what makes it tempting. The tempter has always been a master of 'tailored spiritual ads'.
- Online wolf-attacks are very personal. The key to fending them off is discernment; Jesus met each attack by considering what was on offer and discerning God's answer. We should get used to doing the same.

Wisdom from the Psalms

Hear my voice when I call, Lord;
    be merciful to me and answer me.
My heart says of you, 'Seek his face!'
    Your face, Lord, I will seek.

PSALM 27:7–8

Some questions to think about

1 Your church website is a shop window; how are you using it? What are you advertising… and how's it going? Who is responding?

2 Does your church teach about fake news, alternative facts and clickbait? Where is the most appropriate forum for this?

3 Do you think it morally acceptable for Christian websites to use clickbait? Would you (as a church) use it on your website? Would you (as an individual) post it or approve it on your social media page?

10

Humble, hospitable and generous

The way it is

The church in which I came to faith had a large congregation and very good teaching, but it was the humility, generosity and hospitality of the youth leaders that introduced me to Christ. They 'managed' the youth group every Saturday evening in the church hall, and every Sunday evening, after church, welcomed us into their homes for Bible study. The church was recognised as a 'good church' but what brought me to faith was the generous nature of these leaders – and to this day, the key leader maintains that he never did anything special.

A few years later, when I was a volunteer teacher in Kenya, I hitched a lift in a passing car. I was heading for Nairobi, which was where the driver lived, and when we reached the city outskirts, he asked me where I was staying. I had made no firm plans and he asked if I would like to stay at his home. He was married with children and it was a Christian family. Their home was untidy, noisy and chaotic, and they all just accepted me as a member of their family. In the morning, I packed my rucksack and prepared to go, but at breakfast his wife asked me if I would like to stay another night. I gratefully accepted and the next day she offered again. This time I declined (I felt I'd imposed enough) but as I said farewell, her hand flew to her mouth and with tears in her eyes she apologised to me because she had not offered to wash my laundry. That family would probably not remember me, but my experience of their humility, hospitality and generosity made a major impact on my life because in them (just as in the youth leaders of my home church) I saw a reflection of the character of God.

These experiences were, of course, entirely offline, and the online world is a different kind of place; but if these offline virtues are to be manifested online, it will be in the same manner – one-to-one, and not in a crowd.

Digging deeper

Hospitality was an ancient-eastern virtue. Abraham practised it (for example, when he welcomed strangers into his tent – Genesis 18:2–5), and so did Moses' father-in-law to be, Reuel (Exodus 2:18–20). In the Old Testament, it was embraced by the Hebrews as a religious duty (Leviticus 19:34; Deuteronomy 10:19), and the prophets expected it (2 Kings 6:21–23; Isaiah 58:6–7).

This Hebrew culture of hospitality continued into New Testament times (Luke 7:36; 19:5–6), and Jesus regarded it as normal (Luke 11:5–6), but also encouraged his disciples to extend it to the disadvantaged (Luke 14:13). In the early church, it expressed unity and brought people to faith (Acts 2:46–47), and while it was also practised by the Gentile cultures (Acts 16:15; 28:7), the apostles regarded it as an expression of faith (Romans 12:13; 12:20; Hebrews 13:2), and a sign of someone's single-mindedness for Christ (1 Timothy 5:9–10).

Generosity also runs in a similar biblical seam (Psalm 112:5; Proverbs 11:25; Luke 6:38; 2 Corinthians 9:7), and hospitality and generosity are often interchangeable. In the Old Testament, a common theme linked both virtues: the Hebrews were strangers in a foreign land (Egypt), but God generously freed them and brought them into his land; they should, therefore, welcome strangers themselves and be equally generous. In short, they were expected to reflect the nature of God. This theme (those who were far from God have been welcomed into his kingdom) underlies New Testament attitudes towards generosity and hospitality, with the added dimension of humility as the foundation from which the other two virtues flow.

Humility, in the Christian sense, means having a right view of self. New life in Christ is a work of God, and the Old Testament encouragement to 'remember what God has done for you' remains (Ephesians 2:8–10; 2 Timothy 1:9). It is also made clear, however, that a proper view of self (Romans 12:3) is both a reflection of Christ (Philippians 2:6–8) and a work of God in the individual believer (James 4:6). Therefore, in New Testament thinking, new life in Christ is primary, dependence on Christ is expressed in humility, and lived out through (among other things) generosity and hospitality.

Pause for thought

Churches invest time and energy into preparation for Sunday worship, but how much is invested in a generous, hospitable welcome? While the content of Sunday services is important, it's often the humility, hospitality and generosity of individual church members that brings others to Christ. If you had a choice, where would you choose to invest your time and energy – into better Sunday worship, or in bringing an individual to Christ?

Joining the dots

In most developing countries, hospitality is still an expected cultural response; generosity, however, might be regarded as more of a personal choice. In developed nations, such as Britain, hospitality and generosity are no longer culturally expected, and while people appreciate those who practise these virtues, no one feels obliged to emulate them. Similarly, in the UK, there are generous people who are not hospitable (for example, the wealthy who donate to charity but live in isolation), and (often among the less wealthy) people can be very hospitable without being particularly generous.

The truth is that, in our individualistic culture (see Chapter 5), virtues are regarded as 'individual commodities', exercised from a secular altruism, and largely a matter of personal choice. In this (as in much else), Christianity is countercultural because Christians understand all virtues to be linked to each other, and to God's character. In the current cultural environment of the UK, being hospitable and generous is, therefore, no longer the 'unspoken testimony' it used to be, because those who experience it may well just think, 'You are a great person,' and move on. The link between these virtues and a life-changing relationship with Christ has to be pointed out; then the person has the opportunity to look 'through' the virtuous actions and glimpse the God from whom they flow. In the 21st century, unless Christians make that connection clear, others won't automatically spot it.

In a sense, this makes the 21st century similar to the first century, although for an ironically different reason. In the early church, hospitality was culturally expected, so Christians had to offer a qualitatively different kind of hospitality if it was to reflect the generosity of God. In the 21st century, the same is true, but this time because people have *no* cultural expectations at all!

It's against this cultural backdrop and biblical understanding that humility, hospitality and generosity impact the offline world, but the question is, can these virtues make any impact online?

A way forward

The internet can be an opinionated, tetchy and self-important arena, so an online 'voice' that is humble, hospitable and generous might be expected to receive a warm welcome. In reality, it often doesn't – and for a very good reason. Many people are online because they just want everyone to agree with them… and they think that everyone else going quiet is the same as agreement (more on this in Chapter 17). So, entering an online debate with humility, hospitality and generosity is most likely to be an uphill task. It doesn't mean that Christians shouldn't attempt it, though.

- **Be humble**. You are no better, or worse, than anyone else; everyone is the same before God (Romans 3:23). You are only different by dint of your acceptance of what Christ has done for you (v. 24). Therefore, focus on the needs of others.

- **Be hospitable**. Welcome those who don't agree with you into the discussion. Listen to what they have to say. Let your remarks connect back to your faith. Don't be afraid to say, 'I don't know' or 'I could be wrong.' Encourage everyone to think further. Invite them to stay on, or come back.

- **Be generous**. Look for the best in everyone. Compliment others when it's justified. Circulate good news.

- And pray; always pray; let God in.

The biblical principle

Offer hospitality to one another without grumbling.
1 PETER 4:9

- Keep in mind that, in the offline world, hospitality is most usually experienced one-to-one. Online, head for small chat rooms or individual conversations.

- Keep a right view of self (keep humble). If someone online tells you that you are a lousy person, why not agree with them? After all, you admit that you are a lousy person to God all the time, why would it come as a surprise when someone else notices?

Wisdom from the Psalms

My heart is not proud, Lord,
   my eyes are not haughty;
I do not concern myself with great matters
   or things too wonderful for me.
But I have calmed and quieted myself,
   I am like a weaned child with its mother;
   like a weaned child I am content…
Put your hope in the Lord
   both now and for evermore.

PSALM 131:1–3

Some questions to think about

1 Reflect on why your church is online. Is it primarily to benefit current members, to benefit online visitors, or to advertise? If it helps, work out a 'vision statement' for your church website or social media page and refer to it from time to time.

2 Reflect on why you are personally online. Is it primarily for your own benefit or are you there to benefit others? If it helps, work out a personal 'vision statement' for your online life and refer to it from time to time.

3 Do you have any experience of online expressions of hospitality and generosity leading to offline responses? Can you think of dangers to beware of and opportunities to welcome?

11

A digital sabbath

The way it is

Although referring to any particular report is pointless here (as it will keep being superseded), if you enter 'smartphone usage', or 'smartphone daily hours' (or similar), into your favourite search engine, it will find various reports voicing concerns.

The first concern is the amount of time people spend on their portable devices (with a particular focus on smartphones). Reports show the average minutes or hours different age groups spend interacting online each day, and it's a lot... and for some people, it's *really* a lot. This is a cause for concern because those who spend a lot of time interacting online show signs of being more awkward in offline social settings – and this is especially true for children and young people who do not already have a broad experience of offline social interaction. It might, of course, not mean that online interaction makes for socially awkward offline people; it might mean that socially awkward offline people find the more 'distant' online social interaction easier to handle; and whether the often quasi-social nature of online social media is helpful is debatable. For example, peer pressure among young people often forces them to interact online more than they would choose to, which can cause them to feel trapped in a pattern of life not of their own choosing.

The second concern is that medical reports show that the blue light emitted by screens prevents sleep (use a search engine to browse 'screens and sleep' or similar). This is, again, a particular concern for young people and children who, if they use screens up to the moment when they are expected to drop off to sleep, don't. This then impacts family life when over-tired young people are unready for school or work the next day, and also alters the trajectory of their education and career for the worse.

The third concern voiced by the reports focuses on adult online behaviour which leads to arguments in the offline world. Adults who interact online through their phone when they are in restaurants with their partners or friends offend those they are with. Adults who wake in the night and check their social media or work messages offend the partner who is sharing their bed. This kind of online behaviour causes offline relationships to break down because the offline partner, or friend, feels that the other person is being 'socially unfaithful' by 'leaving' an intimate offline moment to interact with someone more interesting or attractive online – and doing it right in front of the person with whom they supposedly have a special relationship!

Taking the long view, new technology always causes knee-jerk concerns – some of which prove to be valid and some of which do not. The introduction of affordable video recorders in the 1980s, for example, caused a great deal of proper concern about the circulation of unregulated 'video nasties', and in the UK, legislation was introduced to regulate the content of video films. There was also, however, an outcry that the introduction of home-video machines would close all cinemas and destroy the film industry – which never happened… once the movie business noticed that they could release their blockbuster films on video cassettes, and that millions of people would buy them! Go back further into history, and critics of early steam engines feared that their speed would harm women's bodies (and render them infertile); go back even further and there was unrest when pipe-organs replaced minstrels in English churches. Go right back, and very probably, when the bow and arrow was invented, someone in the tribe shook his head, complained that the bow-string hurt his fingers, and predicted dire consequences. New tech always stimulates knee-jerk concerns.

Although smartphones have been around for a while, they (along with tablets) only started to impact the general public somewhere between 2007 and 2009. These portable devices, while ubiquitous, are therefore still comparatively new tech, so it's unsurprising that their impact is not yet completely clear. The way they are being used, however, *is* clear, and some of the concerns are justified. While some people hardly ever access the internet on the move, others are addicted to their device and cannot leave it alone, even for a moment.

What do Christians have to contribute to the portable-device debate? Is there a biblical principle? There is, and it is rooted in an understanding of sabbath.

Digging deeper

The foundation of sabbath is in the creation narrative: 'Then God blessed the seventh day and made it holy, because on it he rested from all the work of creating that he had done' (Genesis 2:3), and this becomes a principle in the ten commandments (Exodus 20:8–11). In keeping the sabbath, God's people reflect the nature of God – he worked for six days and then rested, and they follow the same pattern.

In Judaism, by New Testament times, a plethora of auxiliary rules specified what was (and was not) work on the sabbath. A tailor, for example, must not carry a needle because for him, that was work. A farmer could haul an animal out of a ditch if its life was threatened; but if it was in no immediate danger, it must wait where it was until the next day. A burn could be soothed, but the application of healing ointment must wait until the sabbath had passed… and so on and so forth, until Jesus challenged the auxiliary rules and pointed people back to the sabbath intention, which was to reflect the nature of God. That intention had never gone away (Psalm 118:24), it had just become hidden, because the *details* of how to live obediently had overshadowed the *reason* for living obediently. Obedience had become an outward show instead of an inward reality (Matthew 23:25). Jesus, however, chose to break the auxiliary rules on many occasions; for example, by healing on the sabbath a condition that could reasonably wait until the following day (Mark 3:1–6), and came into conflict with the religious authorities as a result. Jesus, however, proclaimed himself to be Lord of the sabbath (Matthew 12:8).

In the early church, the expectation of sabbath continued (Hebrews 4:9–10), but the apostles clearly believed that the ancillary rules no longer applied, even though many of them had grown up observing them (Philippians 3:7–11). The focus of the sabbath in the Christian church therefore moved away from the negative (don't work) towards the positive (worship God), and contributed to the concept of Sunday as a day of worship that, until the 1970s, still dominated British culture. It is no longer a cultural expectation, however, and Christians must work out for themselves how to keep the sabbath holy when most of their neighbours don't. When it comes to our online life, the question sharpens still further. In what ways do Christian people change their online behaviour on the sabbath to mark that day out as holy to God?

Joining the dots

In a pre-industrial nation, the concept of sabbath is vital for purely sociological reasons. In the Old Testament, only the wealthy enjoyed what we, in Britain today, would recognise as 'leisure time'. Everyone else began work shortly after the sun came up and, apart from a lunch break during the heat of the day, finished work towards the time when the sun went down, every working day; and with only rushlights in their homes, most people slept during the hours of darkness. The sabbath, though, was a day for rest, refreshment, time with family and an opportunity to worship God.

It was also the fourth commandment, which the Hebrew people took very seriously. Josephus (a Jewish historian writing in the first century AD) records that during the Maccabean revolt (167–160BC), Syrian soldiers cornered Hebrew rebels in caves. The rebels were offered an opportunity to surrender but they refused, so the Syrians attacked; but because it was the sabbath day, the rebels refused to fight (because to fight would be work), and they were all slaughtered with no defence. That's how seriously they took not working on the sabbath (see also 1 Maccabees 2:27–37). Similarly, there were occasions when the Romans deliberately attacked Israelite forces on the sabbath, knowing that there would be no resistance, and Jews were not compelled into Roman military service because it was known that, one day a week, they would not fight – no matter what the disciplinary consequences.

In our post-industrial culture, electricity makes 'daylight activities' possible 24 hours a day; seven-day shopping makes one day look very much like any other; and online access enables a 24–7 society. The question is, in what sense can God's people still keep the fourth commandment and keep holy the sabbath day?

If the sabbath is no different to any other day for Christians, then it is likely that this is another aspect of our lives that has been conformed to the world around us (Romans 12:2). If we don't have the self-discipline to make the sabbath different, we are unlikely to manage any kind of 'rule of life' during the rest of the week.

The bottom line is, if we obey the first and second commandments, and God is pre-eminent in our lives, we have a fighting chance of working out how to obey the fourth (and every other) commandment. If our predominant focus is actually, in every practical reality, our online life, we won't.

A way forward

Smartphones have become central to tech-indigenous culture. The ever-present camera engenders confidence because it is a 'witness' to any incident. Photo-sharing gives some the feeling of companionship, and teenagers may develop feelings for their tech normally associated with pets ('I *love* my phone...'). Some people, (and they can belong to any tech-generation) cannot leave their phone alone... ever.

The Bible teaches that if our relationship with God is not pre-eminent, we seek other, substitute relationships to try and fill that void. In our contemporary culture, a relationship with a phone can be that kind of substitute.

If you know that you have allowed your online life to become pre-eminent, don't beat yourself up; these things happen insidiously.

- Consider your daily behaviour. When you are with people in the offline world, are you actually with them, or is half (or maybe all) your attention on your phone? Let others know that they are important by giving them your attention (whether you already know them, or not). If they realise that you regard them as important, they may see in you a reflection of God, to whom they are very important (1 John 4:7).

- Consider fasting from the internet from time to time – not as a negative, difficult thing, but as an opportunity to show God that he is more important than anything (or anyone) else in your life. Expect fasting to be joyful (Zechariah 8:18–19).

Pause for thought

If you develop a weekly and daily personal 'online/offline' regime, you are being countercultural. If you instigate an online/offline regime with your children, it will mark them as different from their peers. Being countercultural (different) carries social consequences, so why would anyone do that? Because 'if you keep your feet from breaking the sabbath and from doing as you please on my holy day, if you call the sabbath a delight and the Lord's holy day honourable, and if you honour it by not going your own way and not doing as you please or speaking idle words, then you will find your joy in the Lord' (Isaiah 58:13–14a).

The biblical principle

You must observe my sabbaths. This will be a sign between me and you for the generations to come, so you may know that I am the Lord, who makes you holy.
EXODUS 31:13

- Consider your sabbath day (this may be Sunday, or for work reasons, another day of the week). It is an expression of God's covenant with you. In what ways will you mark this day as different, online? How will you rest from your usual activity? How will your seventh day reflect the nature of God?

- Consider your weekday routine. Consider making a rule of life, and let others know when you will, and will not, be available to interact with them online – and explain why; it's a sign of your covenant-relationship with God and one of the ways in which you acknowledge his Lordship (Exodus 31:13).

Wisdom from the Psalms

Whoever dwells in the shelter of the Most High
  will rest in the shadow of the Almighty.
I will say of the Lord, 'He is my refuge and my fortress,
  my God, in whom I trust.'
PSALM 91:1–2

Some questions to think about

1   Does your church suggest a rule of online life? Does it tackle the issues of when, and for how long, children use phones and tablets? Does it address the adult issues?

2   How do you differentiate the sabbath in your offline life? How does this extend into your online life? Do you follow any kind of 'rule of life'? Would it be helpful to do so?

3   How does your church use the internet? Do church members expect their leaders to receive and respond to emails and texts immediately, regardless of the day or time? Do ministers expect church members to do the same?

12

Stewards of the grace of God

The way it is

Fallen human beings want to believe that they can make it on their own (without God or anyone else), and succeed in the face of all opposition (and possibly, common sense). Our individualistic culture also equates wealth with success, so those who become wealthy through celebrity (not through any kind of talent, but through celebrity itself) validate the idea that *anyone* can be successful.

In the past, a faintly damning cultural mantra was, 'Jack of all trades; master of none', meaning, 'Okay at most things but excellent at nothing'. The past, however, was a community culture where it was accepted that most people would be average and only a few exceptional. The current cultural mantras are 'No one is good at everything,' and 'Everyone is good at something.' Interestingly, the word 'good' is usually interpreted to mean 'excellent', which is an expression of cultural individualism and the need for everyone to be different from everyone else. Even more interestingly, neither mantra is observably true. Some people *are* actually pretty good at everything (they may not be excellent, but they are pretty good), and some people are actually, not very good at *anything*.

Fallen human beings also love a quick-fix. For example, if someone offers weight-loss pills, people will queue for them, because the promised quick-fix is preferable to the hard, lengthy lifestyle changes (and significant mental shift) needed in order to eat healthily and exercise more. Whether it's medical concerns, relationship problems or anything else, the quick-fix is attractive. In previous, offline generations, con men turned up in marketplaces offering miracle-cure medicines which purported to heal all ills – physical, emotional and mental. These tinctures were usually just laxatives, but the con men moved on while their customers were 'indisposed', and they generally never visited the same town twice! The internet is the new marketplace, and it's full of contemporary cons. Take, for example, the popularity of vlogging nutritionists (many of whom have little in the way of qualifications), sharing their wonder diets. (While a dietician studies for three years to gain an academic degree, anyone can take a quick nutritionist's online course and pay a few pounds for a certificate. The dietician/nutritionist divide is often the difference between an astrophysicist and someone who received a certificate with a telescope they bought.) These online sites gather similar crowds to the old-fashioned offline con men, and their products are not dissimilar! People love a quick-fix, though, and because the internet offers the kind of platform the old-fashioned con men could only dream of, it allows contemporary cons to be presented with a professional gloss.

When the quick-fix is mixed with the cultural mantra (that everyone is good at something) and then blended with current attitudes towards celebrity, the resulting expectation is that a person can just 'be excellent' (at something) without working at it. The Bible, however, takes a different view to the secular mantras and attitudes of every generation, and the biblical truth is, and always has been, that most people who work hard get somewhere even if they are not innately talented.

Nowhere does the Bible suggest that everyone is created with a special talent. Human beings are created in the image of God, but their creation is linked to the task of stewardship (Genesis 1:26). In other words, human beings are created with responsibilities, not talents. What matters is not how talented you are but how you fulfil the responsibilities God has entrusted you with (Matthew 25:14–30). The Bible also teaches that, because of the fall (through human sin), the work required to fulfil those creational responsibilities is hard (Genesis 3:17–19). This biblical understanding flies in the face of contemporary cultural assumptions because money is not a sign of success, fulfilling creational responsibilities is, and… there are no quick-fixes. Christianity is not a quick-fix either, and those who respond to a quick-fix gospel (the promise that if you become a Christian, all your problems will be over) quickly lose their faith. Following Christ is about responding to God's love (John 3:16), doing as God asks by putting our faith in Christ (John 6:29), loving God and others (Hebrews 6:10), and serving as he serves (Matthew 20:27–28). In other words, being a Christian is not about exercising personal talents, but about fulfilling a purpose.

The biblical understanding, then, is that everyone is special – not because they have their own special talent, but because they are loved by God. This is why human family life reflects the nature of God (Ephesians 3:14–15); parents love their children for who they are, not for what they can do, (in fact, they can hate what they do even as they continue to love them!). God does not seem interested in how talented anyone is, only that they use whatever talents they have to fulfil their creational responsibilities (making the earth and the lives of others better than they are). In the New Testament, the understanding is that God, through his Holy Spirit, will give spiritual gifts to every Christian, but that he will deliberately spread these through the church. This is very different from our cultural mantra that 'everyone is good at something'. The Christian understanding is that everyone receives a gift from the Spirit, and everyone is expected to steward that gift appropriately.

Different churches interpret 'spiritual gifts' in different ways and there has been a great deal of thinking about how they should be used offline (including by me[9]). The question under scrutiny here, though, is whether spiritual gifts can and should be used by Christians online. The answer, in part, will depend on our understanding of our creational responsibilities, our purpose in Christ and how we, as stewards, fulfil them.

Digging deeper

Peter says, 'Each of you should use whatever gift you have received to serve others, as faithful stewards of God's grace in its various forms' (1 Peter 4:10). Let's be clear; he is talking about spiritual gifts, not natural talents which people develop as they grow up. Paul helpfully itemised two lists of spiritual gifts; one in his letter to the Romans (12:6–8), and another in his first letter to the Corinthians (12:8–10). Paul probably never meant these lists to be exhaustive or exclusive but they give an idea of the breadth of these gifts. He lists prophecy, serving, teaching, encouraging, contributing to the needs of others, leadership, showing mercy, wisdom, messages of knowledge, faith, healing, miraculous powers, distinguishing between spirits, tongues and the interpretation of tongues.

Some churches will distinguish the 'more supernatural' gifts from the 'less supernatural', some will regard only a few of the gifts in these lists as 'spiritual', and others will regard the 'more supernatural' gifts as only applicable to the early church. However the gifts are interpreted, Paul teaches that they are given by the Holy Spirit (1 Corinthians 12:11), that no one receives them all (v. 8–10: 'to one is given…', 'to another…'), that no gift is more important than any other (vv. 14–27) and that 'we have different gifts, according to the grace given to each of us' (Romans 12:6a). In other words, spiritual gifts are given by God, which gift anyone receives is up to God and the gifts are to be used for the good of others (Romans 12:3–5).

In the offline world, all of these gifts (when exercised) are used by God, but how about in the online world?

Pause for thought

Work your way through Paul's 'gift lists' and ask, in turn, 'Could this gift be exercised online?' Then reflect on whether the Holy Spirit has given you any of the gifts you have identified as 'online gifts' and think about whether you exercise them when you interact with

others online. If you are feeling brave, ask God to show you how (because he will).

The key to using spiritual gifts both offline and online is to understand that God created human beings to fulfil their responsibilities for the earth and its inhabitants in a manner that reflects God (in his image). Christians are a 'new creation' (2 Corinthians 5:17), but this does not simply describe their spiritual state or their heavenly destination. Those newly created are freed from the shackles of the fall (Romans 6:17–18), not only to fulfil their original creational responsibilities but to steward, also, a new-creation responsibility. This is to collaborate with God's desire to see all people become new creations (Matthew 28:18–20). Unless those who are newly created by God use the spiritual gifts he gives them, this new-creation task will be beyond them.

What makes everyone special is that God loves them (John 15:9–17). Christians are not under any pressure to *achieve*, only to *fulfil*, and God makes that possible by giving spiritual gifts. Do you lack faith? That's in the gift list. Are you useless at speaking? Teaching is in the list too; and so is encouraging. God gives different gifts to different people and they take a certain amount of courage (trust in God) to use, but the end result is always the same: spiritual gifts point away from the 'gifted' and towards God because they reflect the one who gave them.

The work of new creation is a work of God. It is nothing any of us can claim credit for (Ephesians 2:8–10). No one is a Christian because they have a talent for it, and no one exercises Christian ministry, in any form, by virtue of their personal ability.

Joining the dots

While the Bible does not teach that everyone is talented, it does teach that everyone is unique and precious (Matthew 10:29–31). Because

God desires a one-to-one relationship with everyone, no one is part of a crowd. No one stands taller than anyone else by dint of their abilities; all are judged according to how they live, not by what they achieve (Luke 16:19–31; Matthew 25:31–46), which means that the only expectations that really matter are the expectations of God.

The internet is a network of people, each of whom is unique. Those with niche interests (who would struggle to find anyone in their offline town who shared them) can link up with individuals across the world with a similar passion. This can, of course, be a bad thing if the niche interest is sinful, but the principle that people can connect online is good, and something Christians can embrace. There is something online for everyone and this means that, whatever online spiritual gift God has given you, there will be somewhere on the internet you can use it, and somewhere God can use you.

A way forward

The New Testament tells us that God gives at least one spiritual gift to every Christian believer. The internet connects people with other people. It is reasonable, therefore, for Christians to expect to use their spiritual gifts online. So, learning how to use spiritual gifts online is as important as learning how to use them offline. To begin, you must accept your new-creation responsibilities and purpose, and recognise your dependence on God.

- Your gifts have been given (they are not natural talents).

- They have been given to serve others (not you).

- They need to be faithfully stewarded (so consider where and how you use them).

- They all point to the grace of God (and away from you).

The hubbub of the online marketplace may not be the right place to exercise spiritual gifts and, if you use them in online shops, you may get hustled out – but in the online places where people discuss, listen and connect on a personal level (mentioned in Chapter 6), don't forget about your gifts. Maybe you can use them. After all, while you and the other people connecting online may be geographically distant from each other, God is present with you all (see Chapter 8).

The biblical principle

Each of you should use whatever gift you have received to serve others, as faithful stewards of God's grace in its various forms.
1 PETER 4:10

The key words are not 'you' or 'gift', but 'serve' and 'steward'.

- If you use the internet for self-promotion, don't use spiritual gifts to raise your profile; that's a misuse, and not what they are for.

- If you dream of exercising spiritual gifts online to become a high-profile online minister, don't be deceived. The kind of spirit that is interested in making you important is not the Holy Spirit.

- If you do not have the gift of discerning between spirits, make sure that you submit your online use of spiritual gifts to someone who does.

Wisdom from the Psalms

Not to us, Lord, not to us
    but to your name be the glory,
    because of your love and faithfulness.
PSALM 115:1

Some questions to think about

1 Does your church expect your online life to fulfil any of your creational responsibilities or your new-creation purpose? Do you? If not, why not?

2 When your church teaches about the gifts of the Spirit, does it assume that they will be used entirely offline? Does the concept of using spiritual gifts online get a mention?

3 God gives gifts to his people for ministry (1 Corinthians 12:7). What are your online gifts? Have you asked for any? (1 Corinthians 12:31).

13

A byte of digital fruit

The way it is

Picture the scene: a person from the tech-indigenous generation arrives in your church one Sunday morning for the first time. They already have a Christian faith and have just moved into your area. Your church has other tech-indigenous people who welcome the new person, and they come again. A church leader makes pastoral contact and quickly realises that the person's past has not been straightforward, but logs this as something to be aware of rather than a cause for immediate concern. The person settles into the church and joins a fellowship group. Like their peers, they live an active online life.

So... that's the scenario. What's your reaction? For some, it will be recognition, because their church, too, has tech-indigenous members who, before they became Christians, made unwise life choices. For others (in churches where this age group is absent), the reaction may be envy.

Let's continue the story. Before long, the person engages in offline behaviour that raises eyebrows among their peers. The church leaders get involved, offline pastoral meetings take place, but the person's offline behaviour escalates exponentially, and so does their online interaction. Their online version of their offline behaviour diverges sharply from the focus of the offline pastoral meetings, and their innumerable posts detail their own edited account of the offline events, while calling into question the integrity of everyone else (involved or not). At the same time, they bombard their peer group with texts, and an older member of the church overhears a conversation between two elderly people in the local supermarket check-out queue which begins with one saying to the other, 'You'll never believe what's happening at the church…' and ends with the version of events the person has posted online. (And, of course, the gossip, by using the phrase, 'You'll never believe…' ensures that their listener will believe every word!)

If you were envious before, are you still envious now? The truth is that churches have a long history of accepting people with demanding needs, and generally churches accommodate them. In the offline past, very demanding individuals tended to focus on church leaders (with phone calls at three o'clock in the morning), or on multiple people who were led to believe that they were the only person with whom the needy individual was having 'confidential conversations'. In the internet age, however, demanding individuals can spend hours each day refining and posting their version of events, and presenting their 'case' to an online 'jury' of (potentially) billions. And, make no mistake, when the online jury is invited to judge your church, it will enthusiastically spread the muck around.

Digging deeper

Paul refers to spiritual fruit as: 'Love, joy, peace, forbearance, kindness, goodness, faithfulness, gentleness and self-control' (Galatians 5:22–23), and spiritual fruit should not be confused with spiritual gifts. Spiritual gifts (see Chapter 12) are given for ministry, and exercising gifts is not so much a matter of development as of learning where, when and how to use them. Think of spiritual gifts as bicycles. They are given 'fully formed' so the recipient just needs to learn where, when and how to ride (the ocean, for example, is an inappropriate place to cycle). Spiritual fruit, however, do not arrive 'fully formed'; they grow within new-creation lives and they take time. The more one-minded a believer is about Christ (see Chapters 7 and 8) the bigger the fruit will grow; the more double-minded, the smaller they remain.

Pause for thought

When spiritual fruit and spiritual gifts are confused, the church is led astray. A gifted preacher, for example, is often assumed by congregations to be automatically 'holy' (with well-developed spiritual fruit). This may, however, be a false assumption, and the preacher's private behaviour may be (shockingly) unholy. Their preaching gift is a gift; nothing more – and it says nothing about the preacher's personal holiness. It's like a bicycle they have been given. They may ride it well and even show off with 'no-hands tricks'; but no one has to be particularly holy to ride a bike.

Jesus said, 'By their fruit you will recognise them. Do people pick grapes from thorn-bushes, or figs from thistles?' (Matthew 7:16). This means that new-creation lives are not recognised by their popularity; nor by their success; and not even by their gifting. They are recognised by their fruit.

- Consider again Paul's list of spiritual fruit (love, joy, peace, forbearance, kindness, goodness, faithfulness, gentleness and self-control). Now go to an online thesaurus and look up the antonyms (opposite) of each of those words. This list will look something like this: hate, despair, discord, intolerance, hostility, dishonesty, treachery, hardness and instability.

- While spiritual fruit feeds reconciliation and peace, the opposite fruit feeds dissention and chaos. Now, consider again the scenario presented at the beginning of this chapter and ask which list (the spiritual fruit or their antonyms) best describes that situation? Look at the fruit, because that tells you about the tree.

In the old, offline world, it was possible for church leaders and congregational members to live double-minded Christian lives. In Western culture, where the secular focus on 'success' was incorporated into Christian thinking, spiritual gifts tended to 'outrank' spiritual fruit to the extent that while public ministries (gifts) were lauded, private lives (fruit) were kept private. In the internet age, the private has a habit of being made public as what is whispered in darkness is shouted from the digital rooftops (see Chapter 1). If this leads Christians to focus more on spiritual fruit than previous generations have, so much the better.

Joining the dots

How do you judge a website or an individual online? What yardstick do you use when landing on a new website, or making first contact? What yardstick do you hope that others will use when they land on your website (or your church's website) or when they message you for the first time?

Most people use popularity (the number of followers, approvals or circulations), the premise being that because this site or person is supported by so many, they must be really good. Sadly, crowds can be wrong, and the size of the crowd says nothing about whether the opinions being expressed are good or bad (consider, as an extreme example, the crowds who turned out to support the Third Reich). This is particularly true for the internet. Do an online search for 'social bots' and you will soon discover that it is possible to buy popularity on various social media platforms. Bots are programmes which give the appearance of human support, and if you do an online search for 'social bots, politicians', you will discover that politicians and political parties use bots to give the appearance of popularity. So, if you use popularity, or the number of circulations or approvals, as your yardstick, be aware that you may just have been conned.

The only true yardstick is the one recommended by Jesus: 'By their fruit you will recognise them,' and it's a yardstick by which you should encourage others to measure you (see Chapters 4, 5 and 7). As a Christian, you have a personal faith, and the size of your spiritual fruit is as personal as it gets.

Be aware, though, that the biblical imagery is much more basic than our 21st-century supermarket-experience of fruit. We are used to uniform, washed, pre-packaged fruit, but to a person living in biblical times, fruit grows on a tree or bush, not to benefit the tree or bush, but to benefit the creature that eats it. The tree or bush, though, gets to spread its seed through the fruit because, when ripe, it either falls off or is picked off and eaten by a bird, a beast or a human being. The seeds travel through the 'host's' digestive system and are then deposited in a nutritious pile of... well, for the sake of decency, insert here: Your Word Of Choice (YWOC, pronounced, 'why-woc'). In these little piles of YWOC, the seeds grow into trees or bushes which produce more tasty and nutritious fruit (and in the case of human YWOC, the seeds may even be helpfully buried – Deuteronomy 23:13).

Human beings are familiar with YWOC. Everyone has YWOC days. For some, family life and relationships turn to YWOC; for others, their working life is truly YWOC. Most people have really YWOC experiences, and sometimes, the whole of life can feel like one big pile of YWOC. But that's where spiritual fruit grows; in the YWOC, and Christians with developed spiritual fruit tend to be those who have willingly waded into the YWOC of life, just as Jesus did.

There are three key biblical facts to understand about spiritual fruit:

- Popularity and fruitfulness are not the same; in fact, in many circumstances, they are mutually exclusive.

- Spiritual fruit exists for the benefit of others. Fruity Christians do not benefit directly from their own spiritual fruit, and those with well-developed spiritual fruit tend to be more aware of their personal failings than those with small fruit, and turn to Christ more regularly (1 Peter 5:6–7; see Chapter 8).

- Spiritual fruit grows in the YWOC of life. If you remove yourself from the world, your fruit will remain small; get into the YWOC and your spiritual fruit will grow (2 Corinthians 6:4–10).

A way forward

If your church has not yet experienced a scenario like that described at the beginning of this chapter, sooner or later it will, as the tech-indigenous generation (and whose children are also tech-indigenous) gradually replace the generations who grew up offline. In British culture, where individuals do not accept church discipline unless they choose to, and do not submit to the gifts of leadership and encouragement unless they decide to, spiritual fruit remains. Facing both offline and online situations armed only with spiritual fruit can feel very 'low-powered', because no human being naturally counters attack by offering fruit! However, offering love, joy, peace, forbearance, kindness, goodness, faithfulness, gentleness and self-control is actually offering a new-creation heart that has been transformed by the power of Christ. Being spiritually fruity is a work of God.

Be aware that, however much fruit you offer, some people just want a fight. These people hope that when they provoke, either you, your church, or your leaders will retaliate. They can then edit your retaliation, publish it online and proclaim themselves to be the attacked and wounded party. If they are looking for a fight and you offer the fruit of the Spirit, they will probably pelt you with rotten fruit until they get bored or tired and go away. So, offer spiritual fruit, but expect to get a face-full, and factor in how much online and offline work will be needed to explain the situation to others. Ask God to grow good spiritual fruit out of the pile of reeking YWOC, though, and trust him. He 'is able to do immeasurably more than all we ask or imagine, according to his power that is at work within us' (Ephesians 3:20).

As a postscript, for those who are curious about how the scenario which began this chapter played out, the situation was hard and hurtful and, in the end, was contained rather than resolved. The person moved on to another church and the online 'details' they posted helped those who wanted to form a negative opinion of the church to form it. The church leaders and members involved, though, came through battered but a little more spiritually fruity, and caused one particular person who heard about it (me) to wonder how Christians might approach online interactions biblically. Where there's YWOC, there's fruit...

The biblical principle

> By their fruit you will recognise them. Do people pick grapes from thorn-bushes, or figs from thistles?
> MATTHEW 7:16

When you are online:

- Bear in mind that the way people use the internet reveals their 'fruit'; and the way you interact online reveals yours.

- Try not to run from or avoid those who exhibit online 'bad fruit'. Instead, see if there are ways in which you can offer good, spiritual fruit into the mix.

- Online, learn how, when and where to exercise the spiritual gift of discernment.

- And, you are still praying before you post, aren't you (see Chapter 2)?

Wisdom from the Psalms

> The righteous will flourish like a palm tree,
>   they will grow like a cedar of Lebanon;
> planted in the house of the Lord,
>   they will flourish in the courts of our God.
> They will still bear fruit in old age,
>   they will stay fresh and green,

proclaiming, 'The Lord is upright;
 he is my Rock, and there is no wickedness in him.'
PSALM 92:12–15

Some questions to think about

1 Reflect on YWOC seasons and situations, and spiritual fruit. When was the last time you deliberately waded into a YWOC situation for the sake of Christ? When did others last remark on your spiritual fruit? Is there a correlation?

2 Reflect on the scenario presented in this chapter. How will your church handle a similar situation when it arises? What part will you play?

3 Think about your online life. Do you avoid online YWOC interactions? Should you?

14

Dealing with digital gossip

The way it is

Look up 'gossip' in any online dictionary; it means to talk destructively about a person's private business or situation, and pass on untruth as fact. In British culture, the stereotypical gossip is an elderly woman but the truth is, while some people gossip more than others, to some extent everyone does it – including children, teenagers and the middle-aged. It's not gender-specific, and it can be initiated with a tiny lift of one eyebrow which changes a firm statement into a cynical question. (For example, end the following sentence with a firm full stop or a subtle question mark: 'He is a wonderful person.') Gossip can be very subtle.

Gossip is tempting because it promises inclusion. Agreement with other individuals, or with a group, creates a bond, and shared secrets strengthen it. It doesn't matter if what is agreed is true or false; it's the agreement itself that makes the bond. Exciting and naughty 'secrets' tighten the bond, but it's the excitement and naughtiness that matters, not the truth. This pair-bonding and group-bonding lies at the heart of all bullying, and is also what makes the lives of victims so terrible – because the truth does not stop it. Bullies are not interested in the truth. They are bound together by their shared secrets (which they probably know are not true), but they don't care, because their social link with each other is more important than the truth. It's what sustains them.

At some point in their life, everyone bonds with another person or with a group through gossip. What is said within the confines of that individual or group relationship destroys the reputation (and possibly even the life) of someone else, but at that moment, the desire to belong is stronger than the desire for fairness, and everyone succumbs. Those who grew up in an offline world will think back to an episode when they were the target of gossip, but also, probably, think back with shame to another episode when they colluded with gossip – and may even have instigated it. Students gossip about other students and their teachers; church members gossip about each other and their leaders; church leaders gossip about the leaders of other churches and their overseers; and so it goes on. Gossip happens because people use it to bond socially.

Gossip is *about* a person and takes place when the person is absent (behind their back). Bullying is directed *at* a person and takes place when the person is present (to their face). The words and sentiments, though, are essentially the same, and so is the motivation. Children bullying other children may appear to be light years away from two elderly people gossiping about their neighbour but, while the offline consequences are different, what is happening is essentially the same. Gossips and bullies bond with one another at the expense of someone else; they are the 'in crowd', their entry fee is paid by the misery of their 'target', and their ticket to get in is gossip.

Pause for thought

For the tech-indigenous generation, the line between gossip and bullying is almost indistinguishable. Gossip is no longer 'behind their offline backs'; it's in their faces on their social media pages, in anonymous messages, and it's everywhere they go because it arrives on every device they use. They cannot escape it at school or college, at home or anywhere else. For tech-indigenous children and teenagers, gossip has turned into bullying and there is nowhere they can escape from it.

Digging deeper

The Bible expresses a clear and consistent view about gossip. Here are a few examples:

- 'Do not spread false reports. Do not help a guilty person by being a malicious witness' (Exodus 23:1).

- 'Do not go about spreading slander among your people. Do not do anything that endangers your neighbour's life. I am the Lord' (Leviticus 19:16).

- 'Without wood a fire goes out; without a gossip a quarrel dies down. As charcoal to embers and as wood to fire, so is a quarrelsome person for kindling strife. The words of a gossip are like choice morsels; they go down to the inmost parts' (Proverbs 26:20–22).

- 'Those who consider themselves religious and yet do not keep a tight rein on their tongues deceive themselves, and their religion is worthless' (James 1:26).

The fundamental truth behind all biblical thinking about gossip is that words destroy lives just as surely as weapons destroy bodies. It is, in effect, a way of bullying a person when they are not there. The ninth commandment is: 'You shall not give false testimony against your neighbour' (Exodus 20:16). Gossip breaks this commandment, and those false, destructive words rob others of their quality of life (Proverbs 11:9a), just as surely as a sneaky sword-thrust can rob them of life itself (Exodus 20:13).

The person targeted by gossip is a creation of God, but the gossip demeans, degrades and isolates them. Those who gossip, therefore, disagree with God's pronouncement that human beings are 'very good' (Genesis 1:31). They insinuate the opposite and, because they judge when only God should judge (James 4:12), they set themselves up in the place of God. Their gossip is an expression of original sin (the most basic of all sins), and indicates a life lived in rebellion to God. Their gossip is usually accompanied by other destructive attitudes and behaviours, which is why, in the New Testament, it is often included in a list of sins rather than singled out – because, when a person willingly sins, sin flows through every facet of their life (Romans 1:29–32).

Gossip is not harmless. It harms not only the target (by making their life miserable), but it harms the gossips too, because it separates them from God.

Joining the dots

Gossiping online is easy; with one click you can pass on a lie as if it were the truth. All you have to do is circulate an unsubstantiated remark or post. Something appears in your social media feed (maybe about a person or organisation you know; maybe about a politician or media star); it's malicious but you don't check the content to see if it's true, and maybe it confirms your existing opinion about that person or organisation. You don't think about it; you just read it, snigger and circulate it. And… you feel good, because you have just affirmed your social bond with others who have circulated the post – at the expense of the target person or organisation. You are an online gossip.

Let's think again about the scenario presented in the previous chapter (Chapter 13). The person at the centre of the scenario was not a gossip; they did not interact with others or even respond in any meaningful way. They used the internet to broadcast their story to anyone who would listen and their online activity was a means of publication. Those who received their version of the story and passed it on, however, *were* gossips. They did not check the story or even ask any basic questions; they just accepted it and passed it on, adding their own horror, disgust and indignation to the mix as they did so. Gossiping online is easy.

So, what do you do if you, or your church, become the target of online gossip?

- Understand that gossips are not interested in the truth. Their desire for social bonding is stronger than their desire to know the truth.

- You can choose to turn the other cheek and wait for the gossip to die down (Matthew 5:39).

- You can challenge outrageous accusations, but prepare for a marathon, because you will end up replying to one-sentence accusations with multi-paragraph explanations. Your explanations will, in turn, attract more one-sentence damnations which will also need multi-paragraph replies… and so on. So, if you are going to reply, plan to spend a lot of time replying.

- Remember that gossip thrives when a target is isolated. You are not alone and neither is your church. If you, or your church, become a target of online gossip, 50 church members replying, or ten local churches remarking, can make quite a dent in the gossip's claims. Refutations from many people are more effective than many refutations from one. You are a citizen of the kingdom of God (Ephesians 2:19), so ask the other citizens for help.

- Recognise that the online gossip campaign may end badly for you and your church. Accept the YWOC and trust God anyway (Romans 8:35–39). In the end, your hope is that your online antagonists will meet with God in a new way; and if you get crucified online as part of that process… so be it (2 Corinthians 12:10).

Only a firm social bond with God stops gossip dead, because then the person has no need to bond socially at the expense of others; they already have the most secure bond in creation (Hebrews 6:19). Gossip is a spiritual problem. A changed spirit is the only solution.

A way forward

The internet is not a private world; it's a public forum. This means that when you interact with others online, you cannot necessarily choose who you interact with, and bullying and social exclusion are only a click or two away. You can steward your own online interactions, be prayerful and positive, and still end up slipping into gossip or becoming the target of it. The way forward, in both cases, is the same. Make yourself accountable to others:

- Ask someone to review your public online posts and contributions from time to time. Submit to their assessment (Ephesians 5:21).

- If you slip into becoming an online gossip; repent and apologise (1 John 1:9).

- If you become a target, ask others for help. If possible, explain (offline) to your fellowship group, your church or to other local churches what is going on (Galatians 6:2). Ten minutes of offline conversation can save thousands of online words.

'You are the body of Christ, and each one of you is a part of it' (1 Corinthians 12:27). Don't be deceived into thinking that you are alone or that your online activities have nothing to do with those with whom you share your faith (the church). We are all in this together, so submit to one another and support one another. That is the way of love that reflects the life of God in human beings (1 Corinthians 13).

The biblical principle

Do not let any unwholesome talk come out of your mouths, but only what is helpful for building others up according to their needs, that it may benefit those who listen.
EPHESIANS 4:29

- Always take the long view and remember: taking up your cross daily involves crucifixion. When this happens, you are in the right company (Jesus).

- Seek your validation in God, not in the transitory social bonds formed by gossip (Hebrews 4:16).

- And, if you are an online gossip yourself: stop.

Wisdom from the Psalms

Lord, who may dwell in your sacred tent?
    Who may live on your holy mountain?
The one whose way of life is blameless,
    who does what is righteous,
    who speaks the truth from their heart;
whose tongue utters no slander,
    who does no wrong to a neighbour,
    and casts no slur on others;
who despises a vile person
    but honours those who fear the Lord;
who keeps an oath even when it hurts.
PSALM 15:1–4a

Some questions to think about

1 If your church becomes the target of an online gossip campaign (for the first time or again), are you prepared? Consider developing an action plan, based on biblical principles, to deal with it, and take time to explain it to church members.

2 If an individual in your church becomes the target of an online gossip campaign, are you prepared? Again, consider developing an action plan which can be rolled out immediately to support any church member who finds themselves in such a situation.

3 Does your church initiate safe discussions with children and young people about the realities of their online and offline lives, and the blurred line between gossip and bullying? Can they ask for help, knowing that they will be understood?

15

Dealing with persecution

The way it is

It's tempting to think of persecution as gossip or bullying 'to the max'. The truth is, though, that the motivation is different. Gossips and bullies have no personal interest in their target; anyone will do and any reason is as good as any other. Their aim is to bond with each other at the expense of their target. Persecutors, however, have a very personal interest in their target – they hate them, and their motivation is nothing less than their destruction. While gossips and bullies nip at the heels of their victims, hoping to trip them and share a laugh when they fall, persecutors go for the jugular. Persecution is therefore nearer to the sixth commandment ('you shall not murder') than to the ninth ('you shall not give false testimony against your neighbour'). Gossip is often casual and unconsidered. Persecution is targeted and deliberate.

Online persecutors have a name – trolls – and in the UK, legislation is evolving to deal with online persecution in offline courts. The law, however, usually only comes into play once offences have been committed, which means that victims have to live through the persecution, often for many months or even years before the perpetrator can be arrested and charged. Happily, for most ordinary people, trolls tend to target high-profile individuals, but it's worth thinking through how your church could help and support such an individual.

Most online persecution, though, is not perpetrated by individuals (trolls), but by the online mob. For example, in recent years, when certain individuals have been offered jobs, the announcement has been met with such an online howl of disapproval that the job offers have been withdrawn. Whether the original appointments were wise, or even appropriate, is not the issue – the point is that those who opposed the appointments whipped up such an online storm of protest that the appointments committees backed down. The lesson has been clear; if you don't like something, as long as you make enough noise, you can get what you want. In the old-fashioned, offline world, this would involve leaving your house, lighting a torch and taking to the streets. Now all you need to do is log on.

In essence, the online challenge is nothing new. 'The only thing necessary for the triumph of evil is that good people do nothing' (a quote attributed to a number of different people). Where there is a culture of corporate apathy, or fear, linked with any personal unwillingness to step into the line of fire, the internet allows individuals with loud voices to gain a volume they don't deserve. At rock bottom, if *you* do not stand against the digital roar, the online mob will inevitably get its own way.

Digging deeper

Jesus said, 'Greater love has no one than this: to lay down one's life for one's friends' (John 15:13). So, there's the central, spiritual question, right there. Would you risk becoming the target of a troll or the online mob, and effectively give up your online life, for the sake of someone else? When the next howl goes up about some decision that has been made, will you remark, even if it risks the mob turning on you?

What if you agree with the sentiments of the mob (or perhaps even the troll)? What if it's their actions you disapprove of rather than their viewpoint? Do you just keep quiet? Well, if you want evil to flourish, yes; if you don't, then no. Jesus said, 'Love your enemies and pray for those who persecute you' (Matthew 5:44), and he either meant it or he didn't. If your enemies are being persecuted, then ignoring their plight cannot be described as love and, if you are yourself being persecuted, then the least you can do is pray for your persecutor(s) – and your prayer should be for their benefit, not for your personal relief (Luke 23:34). In other words, you pray that God will bless them, forgive them (Ephesians 4:32) and bring them into a closer relationship with Christ; not that God will change the whole situation to make your personal life more comfortable. The former is what Jesus did (Luke 22:42) and what he commands us to do: 'Whoever wants to be my disciple must deny themselves and take up their cross daily and follow me' (Luke 9:23). The cross is where Jesus gave up his life for the sake of others, and the cross Christians are called to take up daily is of the same kind. We give up our lives for others.

In an internet age, this understanding of discipleship gives our online life a very particular spiritual edge. Online interaction is not a 'holiday' from our faith (time off for leisure); it is a 'holy day' where our spirituality is central because, at any point, we may find ourselves with a choice: log off, keep quiet and allow evil to thrive, or interact, speak up and maybe sacrifice our online life for the sake of another. It's a tough choice.

Pause for thought

For the tech-indigenous generation, the line between bullying and sexual abuse (by their peers) has become almost indistinguishable. Access to online porn is shaping the sexual understanding and expectations of even young children, and leading them to abuse other children offline, while the immediacy and intimacy of texts and social media ramp up cultures of social exclusion and bullying. To gain insight into this, search 'children abusing children' (and don't worry, this search won't leave you with an undesirable browser history; the first few pages list reports from the NSPCC, the NHS, *The Independent*, the BBC and so forth). Be aware that for thousands of British children and young people, persecution through peer sexual abuse is a daily reality.

Joining the dots

Most mature adults will never experience a troll directly, but it's worth recognising who in your church might. Single adults from the tech-assimilator generation can be vulnerable to manipulative predators, but your tech-indigenous members will already have experienced some degree of online persecution – and the culture they inhabit can invade the church. So, if you do not address 'all that nastiness' with children because you think that if you raise it, you will destroy their innocence, wake up. Online persecution may already be part of their daily lives and your well-meaning silence may end up protecting their persecutors.

Your main church leader can also become a target. In the eyes of some, their role gives them a high-enough profile to make them a worthy target for their hate. If this happens, it is unlikely that the 'level' of trolling will reach illegal levels (death threats and the like); it is more likely to be a relentless, complaining diatribe that just goes on and on and on… For your church leader, it will not be like facing a life-threatening disease; it will be more like living with a constant low-grade infection. Peter says, 'Each of you should use whatever gift you have received to serve others, as faithful stewards of God's grace in its various forms' (1 Peter 4:10), so think through how your church can support your leader if a troll makes them their target.

When individuals act criminally, the courts seek to determine if the criminal is mentally unstable. The shorthand phrase is: are they mad or bad? In the online world, this phrase can be extended: is the individual mad, bad or sad? Internet trolls often turn out to be very sad people who use their online 'power' to sublimate their offline inadequacy. Similarly, the obsessions of the mentally unstable can cause a great deal of online grief to others, and online interaction allows bad people to behave appallingly from a safe distance.

The internet offers everyone the same opportunity, regardless of whether they are obsessive, aggressive, inadequate, generous or loving. The whole of humanity is out there and, once you log on, who knows who is sitting on the other side of your screen? It could be a saint or someone who is sad, mad or bad. Your focus, though, is not their condition, because Christ loves them every bit as much as he loves you (John 3:16). Your focus is whether or not you can point them towards Christ (Matthew 28:18–20). If you can, then the persecutor's life will change (look what happened to Saul when he met Jesus – Acts 9:1–19), and if you can't, then you may need to find a way to shake the digital dust off your feet and move on (Matthew 10:14).

If your church, or someone from the tech-immigrant or tech-assimilator generation, becomes the target of online persecution, it is less likely to come from an individual, but through a crowd. Perhaps you are undertaking a renovation project which will change the look of your church building, or altering a long-standing pattern or style of worship. Perhaps your church is planning a charitable project, such as helping young offenders or offering assistance to the homeless. Perhaps your church is responsible for a community amenity, such as a graveyard. In many neighbourhoods, active expressions of faith attract criticism from those who, for whatever reason, hold strong views and don't like what the church is doing, or how it's doing it. At this point, individuals can use the internet to bombard the church, or the church leader, into submission. All it takes is one or two mob-minded people to get the ball rolling and the online gossips will do the rest. Make no mistake; whatever the purported intent, this is persecution – and if you have any doubt, look at the motivation of those who set the mob running. They hate what is happening; they hate you and your church for doing it; their intention is to go for the jugular, hurl you and your church to the ground, and get their own way.

The fact that contemporary persecutors use the internet as their medium (rather than flaming torches and clubs) allows them to declare innocently, 'All I did was express an opinion.' God forgive them. No, literally, '*God, forgive them*' – that is your prayer, and it is prayed for their benefit, not yours. If you seek to follow Christ, expect to be crucified, if not daily, at least from time to time.

A way forward

Persecution is part of Christian life. Jesus was persecuted (John 11:53), so was Paul (Acts 9:23–24), and countless Christian people have been persecuted down the ages and across the world. It still goes on today. It may not be apparent in your street, or even in your town, because after 1,500 years of Christianity, Britain is a great place to live. Go online, though, and you soon dip down through the cultural veneer into the reality of what people personally believe and think.

Online persecution is a reality, and although the 'online' part is new, the 'persecution' isn't. It's simply a digital expression of what Jesus warned his disciples to expect. The 21st-century disciple's choice is the same as the choice faced by disciples in every previous offline age: focus on Christ and interact, or focus on self and run away.

- Christians are called to forgive and to seek reconciliation. Where both (or all) parties are open to this, the results are life-changing. Where it is resisted, Christians are still called to forgive, but reconciliation becomes impossible – but that is between the person who refuses to be reconciled and God. Think of it as the 'Ezekiel principle' (Ezekiel 3:17–19): if you don't speak, God holds *you* accountable; if the other party will not listen, God holds *them* accountable.

- You can't live another person's life for them. Your task is to live your own life in obedience to Christ and address issues as and when you come across them (2 Corinthians 10:5). And, when you address them, don't be surprised if you walk into a YWOC-storm (John 15:18).

The biblical principle

> Blessed are those who are persecuted because of righteousness, for theirs is the kingdom of heaven.
> MATTHEW 5:10

- Try not to fear YWOC-storms. When you challenge the behaviour or attitudes of others, you may well be challenging someone who is closed to God. Engaging spiritually is then like entering a battle. As Paul says, 'Our struggle is not against flesh and blood, but against the rulers, against the authorities, against the powers of this dark world and against the spiritual forces of evil in the heavenly realms' (Ephesians 6:12). If you interact spiritually online, your struggle is with worldly darkness and spiritual resistance. Online trolls, mobs and persecutors spearhead the counter-attack.

- You do not interact in order to win battles. You interact with people, powers and spiritual forces because your focus is God's kingdom.

- And if you, yourself, have slipped into joining the online mob: go home.

Wisdom from the Psalms

> Set a guard over my mouth, Lord;
>   keep watch over the door of my lips.
> Do not let my heart be drawn to what is evil
>   so that I take part in wicked deeds
> along with those who are evildoers;
>   do not let me eat their delicacies.
> PSALM 141:3–4

Some questions to think about

1 Are you ready to stand for Christ online? Are there online issues your church should involve itself with? Are there high-profile individuals who need your support and help? Who will organise your church's response, and how?

2 Are you prepared to help one another, or your church leaders, if they become the target of online persecution or an internet mob? Could you develop an action plan which could be rolled out immediately should it be needed?

3 Does your church encourage safe arenas where children and young people can talk about the blurred line between online bullying and offline sexual abuse? Do they know that they can ask for help and get it?

16

Stewards of a digital footprint

The way it is

In the comparatively recent past, unless a person had cash with which to pay for the daily necessities of life (or were a criminal using false identities), their 'footprints' in the offline world could be followed every time they wrote a cheque or used a credit card or cash machine. It was not a precise method of detection, but it indicated roughly where the person was living, noted any repeated patterns of behaviour and gave an idea of where those with the legal right to look might find someone.

In recent years, things have moved on. Smartphones contain location trackers (used by apps to navigate your route, suggest restaurants near your location and so forth). If you have not switched this feature off (on every app that tracks you), the authorities have only to turn on your phone to find out where you have been, and when, or to contact your ISP to find out where you are. You can use software (that you have downloaded and installed) to 'shred' your browser history, but this only means that the authorities cannot track your past through that device. Your ISP still knows exactly which websites you have visited and when, and the websites themselves know which pages you looked at ('cookies' gather this information and your browser passes them back to the server), so if you are 'a person of interest' to the authorities, it won't take them long to find your online footprints.

In many ways, this technological tracking is reassuring, because it means, for example, that terrorist plans can be foiled before atrocities occur. There are, however, civil liberty concerns which centre on whether the authorities using this tech are trustworthy and have the best interests of their citizens as their prime concern. Repressive governments use the new tech to repress, and even the noblest civil authorities are not entirely free from self-interest. However, considering a biblical approach to governmental online policy is beyond the scope of this book; the focus here is more personal.

Online tracking is moving on (yet again). Online payments were initially introduced by banks or online payment systems (such as Paypal), which all used the same business pattern. They took a small commission on every payment made, which is how they made their money. The banks then extended this into offline payments by introducing contactless cards to replace cash. Cash costs banks money because it has to be collected, shipped, counted, guarded and secured. Contactless payments earn banks money, because every time a contactless card is used, the bank gets a small commission. The deal with banks and payment systems, though, is that the commission makes them money and they keep the details of your transactions confidential. If the authorities wish to look at your payment footprints, they must obtain a court order. All this will be in the terms and conditions you agreed to, and signed, at some point (as will a tick-box or two giving or denying permission for the bank or payment company to pass on some of your details to other businesses).

This is becoming old news, and new online systems are being developed by the tech companies (for example, at the time of writing, Android Pay and Facebook Payments). To the user, these online methods of payment seem indistinguishable from the systems used by the banks and payment companies, but their basis is different. The tech companies do not take any commission; the service is 'free'. Instead, you give them permission to 'mine' your purchase data, and all data *associated* with your purchase. Look in the terms and conditions. Your data (your online spending of what, where, when and why) is what makes money because 'tech companies really see data as the new oil, and payment data is probably the best quality oil in the business. What they can do with it is endless.'[10] Payment data is what funds the internet because it hands over your digital footprints to businesses who want your custom, and gives them permission to advertise personally to *you*.

Pause for thought

In the 1960s, an elderly relative in my family always brushed her hair and put on tidy clothes before turning on her TV. She kind-of-knew that the people she was watching through her screen were not watching her back, but she didn't want to be caught out – just in case. At the time, my family thought this hilarious, but actually, she was ahead of us. If her screen had been connected to the internet she would have been absolutely right, because someone would always have been watching her back – and how many of us who kind-of-know that, ever actually remember it?

Your device screen is a two-way window. You may be looking through your screen at text, pictures and people in complete offline privacy – but online, someone else is always looking back. The question for Christian people is: when these companies or individuals track your digital footprints back through the online sand to your screen and look through, what do they see? As Izabella Kominska puts it, 'Payment data is a comprehensive record of how you spend and live your life. There's no cheating it.'[11]

Digging deeper

Paul tells Titus to 'remind the people… to slander no one, to be peaceable and considerate, and always to be gentle toward everyone' (Titus 3:1–2). That may not be the intention of many who go online, but it can be the intention of every Christian. Hopefully, most Christians will want to approach their online interactions in this fashion for no other reason than to make the internet a better place.

There is, however, a more personal dimension to every online life. Our online footprints will show any disparity between our publicly professed faith and our personal, private opinions or desires. Jesus had a word for this 'disparity'; he called it hypocrisy. 'On the outside you appear to people as righteous but on the inside you are full of hypocrisy and wickedness' (Matthew 23:28). In an online age, hypocrisy is probably easier to spot than at any pervious time in history and, if we are double-minded Christians (see Chapters 7 and 8), expect others to notice and shout it from the digital rooftops (see Chapter 1). The exposure of hypocrisy, however, while it might be uncomfortable, is probably a good thing, especially if it leads to repentance and changed lives (1 John 2:1–2).

Above the public and below the personal, though, is the spiritual. Paul says, 'Do you not know that your bodies are temples of the Holy Spirit, who is in you, whom you have received from God? You are not your own; you were bought at a price. Therefore, honour God with your bodies' (1 Corinthians 6:19–20). He says this in the context of offline sexual immorality, which, of course, has a direct application to online pornography and hook-up sex sites – but it's also not unreasonable to extend the image. In the offline past, it was common for people to look at one another and to ask, 'What's going on in your head? What's happening behind your eyes?' On the internet, online interaction provides graphic, evidential insight.

So, think of your device screen as a two-way window. From your side, you look out of your body (which as a Christian is a temple of the Holy Spirit), and into an online world and life. From the other side of the screen, every tech-company, business and legal agency looks back at you, along with every individual with whom you are connected through social media (and so forth). As they look back through that two-way window, do they look into a temple of the Holy Spirit? As Izabella Kominska says, there's no cheating what they see; they see *you*. 'Just as he who called you is holy, so be holy in all you do; for it is written: "Be holy, because I am holy"' (1 Peter 1:15–16).

Joining the dots

The internet hosts many legal but unsavoury sites – and each one is just a click away. This can make online interaction a sticky trap for the unwary, or for those with no personal code of stewardship. But for those who are spiritual, 'since we live by the Spirit, let us keep in step with the Spirit' (Galatians 5:25). The personal challenge is to make sure that our digital footprints lead to and from a temple of the Holy Spirit; that our online life is not hypocritically different to our Christian profession of faith (Galatians 6:8); and that posting online is as much an 'act of worship' as praying in church (Romans 12:1).

This does not mean that our online interactions must consist only of Bible quotes, hymns and worthy remarks, and neither does it mean that we only ever visit Christian websites. The word 'worship' derives from 'worth-ship', meaning to give worth to something. In its Christian meaning, the worship of God is about acknowledging God's worth – which we do in church when we pray and worship, but also throughout our lives by acknowledging his life-changing work in us (Philippians 2:13), and its purpose (Ephesians 2:10).

Even if it were possible, in a data-mining online world, for the general public to engage in 'private' web-surfing, it would not be possible for Christian people. God knows where our online footprints lead, is aware of every conversation and mouse click, understands when we are tempted to stray on to sites that are unhelpful, and desires only one outcome: the very best for us (Jeremiah 29:11). The Christian's task is simple to sum up, even if hard to always remember. Whether we are online having fun or engaging in serious discussion, shopping or selling, working or relaxing, chatting or listening, whatever we are doing, God has made us into a temple of the Holy Spirit, and that's what anyone looking back at us through our screen should see.

A way forward

Be spiritual; keep your temple swept and ready for visitors (1 Corinthians 16:13), but be yourself; then you allow others to see the work God is doing in you (Ephesians 2:10).

- Consider your online 'leisure' footprints (maybe the games you play or the movies you stream) and take stock. Are they appropriate to play or show in a spiritual temple (Philippians 4:8)?
- Be honest with others. Confess online mistakes to those you trust; adult to adult; adult to child; church leader to congregation. No one gets life 100 per cent right and everyone needs the forgiveness of God (Romans 3:23–24). Without a culture of appropriate confession (see Chapter 5), hypocritical secrecy becomes a blanket under which sin multiplies. Appropriate confession opens up honest conversations and new life (James 5:16).
- If you stumble across the hypocrisy or online sin of someone else, 'you who live by the Spirit should restore that person gently. But watch yourselves, or you also may be tempted' (Galatians 6:1).

The biblical principle

Do you not know that your bodies are temples of the Holy Spirit, who is in you, whom you have received from God? You are not your own; you were bought at a price. Therefore, honour God with your bodies.

1 CORINTHIANS 6:19–20

In the UK, films receive a 'classification' to guide viewers as to their suitability. Businesses looking at you through your screen will not judge your online life (but they will 'classify' it in order to offer you 18+, PG or U products), but individuals who connect with you through websites and social media will. It may be helpful, as a Christian believer, to reflect on your personal online life and give it an honest 'classification'. Is it suitable for a temple of the Holy Spirit?

There are posts I look forward to reading online (whatever the subject) from certain people. It's not what they say, or even how they say it, and it's not even about the topics on which they choose to post; it's about them. They probably think of themselves as the biggest sinners in creation, with little to offer anyone else, but when I read their contributions, their digital footprints track back through the shifting sands of the internet and I know that I'm looking through my screen into a spiritual temple – and I never fail to be entertained, encouraged, challenged and uplifted all at the same time.

Wisdom from the Psalms

Lift up your heads, you gates;
    lift them up, you ancient doors,
    that the King of glory may come in.
Who is he, this King of glory?
    The Lord Almighty –
    he is the King of glory.
PSALM 24:9–10

Some questions to think about

1 Does your church mention online activity when it teaches about hypocrisy? In its thinking about living consistent lives for Christ, does it mention the internet?

2 Do you have a view about data mining? Does your church? Is this a business practice to be accepted or challenged?

3 Does your church (or do you) help children and young people to understand that they are already leaving digital footprints in the online sand? Do they understand that some footprints could bring their online explorations to the attention of legal agencies and stay with them for the rest of their lives?

17

Me in my small corner

The way it is

'Everyone agrees with me; everyone says the same!' It's a sentiment now commonly expressed, and it's a direct consequence of social media interaction. Because social networks connect like-minded individuals, online networks 'self-seduce' users into thinking that everyone agrees with them. This can be true of political opinion, religious belief, scientific theory, local offline issues and even the 'interpretation' of the law (when someone has committed a crime but wants to believe they haven't). Because people are not connected in any way with those who disagree with their point of view, they therefore believe that *everyone* thinks as they do... until an offline election, the courts or simple facts prove just how wrong their assumption has been. They discover that their online life led them to believe that their opinion was the only opinion, when it actually occupied only a small corner of a very wide gamut.

There is a scientific term called 'confirmation bias'. It's what happens when a scientist begins with a theory and then interprets their research in a way that confirms it, instead of studying the research objectively to see what it *actually* suggests. In other words, because they have already decided what they want to find, that's what they find... even when it isn't there. Confirmation bias describes why so many people were stunned by the results of both the UK referendum and US presidential election in 2016. These voters were confident in (what they imagined to be) indisputable outcomes, because their social network contacts all confirmed their pre-existing bias. Unfortunately for them, their expectations were also completely unfounded, and the outcomes were hard for many to bear. How could this happen, when 'everyone agreed with them'? Confirmation bias is about the most widespread pitfall lurking in all online interaction.

One hundred years ago, most people lived their whole lives within the same community of people, many of whom held different opinions on any and every subject. Across the developing world, this is still true for millions, although the move from agrarian to city life is changing this. In the UK, over the last six generations, improved standards of living have increasingly allowed people to move from one community to another and into neighbourhoods where they feel more comfortable. (To put it bluntly, birds with similar educational, wealth and expectation feathers have flocked together.) Within those offline communities, though, opposing views still exist and, while some of life's difficulties can be moved away from, no one has ever lived in a community where everyone agrees about everything. The internet, however, has changed all that. Now, wherever people live, they connect online, and tend to connect only with those who agree with them – and suddenly, there are no opposing views to wrestle with or debate; there is only mutual agreement and confirmation bias.

How you deal with online difficulty will, in large part, reflect how you deal with offline difficulty, and how you deal with difficulty offline will indicate where, in reality, your community is. Here are five questions to consider:

- How do you handle personal abuse – perhaps when it is hurled at you in the street or in a pub?
- How do you handle political or ideological debate when you are talking with someone who holds very different opinions to you?
- How do you deal with ignorance in others, who for lack of education know less than you?
- How do you ensure that you get along with people you don't like and who don't like you?
- When someone in your neighbourhood or in your church offends you, how do you sort it out?

If your answers to these questions are 'I don't get abused; everyone I know holds the same opinions as me; I say nothing when less educated people express ridiculous opinions; I'm polite to people I don't get on with but I ignore or avoid them; I ask the authorities or my church leaders to sort out problem people for me', then I predict that you are a British Christian; most of your friends are Christians (and probably members of your church); you either stay within the confines of the community in which you live or travel through communities that make you feel uncomfortable to reach community events in areas where people share your values. I also predict that if you have a testimony of God working through you to bring someone to Christ, it will be historical (it happened a long time ago); and that most (if not all) of your online contacts will be people who agree with you and with whom you agree. I'm sorry to have to break this to you, but you are in your small corner… where your bias is constantly confirmed.

I am happy to be proved wrong, so do tell me why my prediction is absolute nonsense – but why would I predict this? Because if your answers are as I suggest, it means that you don't, actually, get out much (that is to say, into the areas of life where most people who as yet have no faith live), and you are probably not mixing in any personal way with anyone who disagrees with you. Young people mix offline all the time; they have no choice; they are packed into classrooms and lecture halls with people they would not choose to associate with. Those of working age have offline work colleagues, but the focus of their working life is their work, so they may not have much opportunity for personal conversation and their company may discourage political or religious discussion. Those in retirement get to choose who they mix with, but tend to choose the quiet life (and, to be honest, more than a few of us are looking forward to that quiet life!).

The question every Christian must answer before God, though, is this: when Jesus commissioned his disciples (Matthew 28:18–20), was that a commission to live a quiet life among those who agreed with them? Was it a commission to hold a faith-candle in a corner, or a commission to set the world ablaze?

Digging deeper

Jesus used the imagery of light to explain his own mission. In his time, during the Feast of Tabernacles (Sukkot), four huge oil-filled lamps, which were located above the women's court of the temple in Jerusalem, lit the city all through the night as a reminder of how God had guided his people through the wilderness with a pillar of fire (Exodus 13:21). Jesus was in Jerusalem during this festival (John 7:1–14) when he said, 'I am the light of the world. Whoever follows me will never walk in darkness, but will have the light of life' (John 8:12). Not only does his claim connect with God's provision to a (historical) journeying people who were lost, and offer a similar light to those seeking to follow God in the present, it's not beyond the bounds of probability that Jesus spoke these words at night in the full glow of those Sukkot braziers. He certainly spoke his words 'to the people', rather than privately to his disciples, and one can imagine the people standing in that crowd, bathed in the brightest light they had ever seen at night, maybe even feeling its heat on their faces, when Jesus' voice cried out – drawing their attention away from the temple and directing it to himself.

That's what light does: it enables you to see clearly anything previously hidden by darkness; and Jesus was absolutely clear that he was the light of the world and that his disciples would be too (Matthew 5:14).

Pause for thought

Victorian author Susan B. Warner wrote the children's hymn 'Jesus bids us shine', which includes the lines: 'Jesus bids us shine with a pure, clear light; like a little candle burning in the night; in this world of darkness, we must shine; you in your small corner, and I in mine.'[12] Popular in America and the UK, this four-verse song affirmed cultures in which Christianity was the norm and where, amid the general blaze of faith, even children could contribute their own small flame. Over the subsequent six generations, however, while the general blaze of Christian witness declined, Christian children continued to grow into adults who believed that all God required of them was to 'glimmer in their own corner', which for many meant within the privacy of their own thoughts and in church. Twenty-first century adults are not Victorian children. It's time for Christians to stop shielding faith-candles in corners and to hold aloft faith-torches in public (Matthew 5:14–16) – and the internet is a place of public engagement.

Joining the dots

During the previous chapters of this book, some readers may have grown increasingly uneasy about online interaction. The internet can be a scary, dangerous and challenging place, and some readers may at this point be thinking, 'I'll retreat into the "safe" arenas.' If it were up to us, that's what we'd all do – after all, the land of online confirmation bias is a lovely place (until offline reality intrudes and kicks us where it hurts). Our problem (if it is a problem) is that, if we take the Bible seriously and apply biblical principles to our online interaction, we have no choice but to engage. It is what God asks of us. Jesus' commission in Matthew 28 tells us, in effect, to 'go to people everywhere'. And who is online? People; everywhere... and we 'go' to them because most of them won't come to us. Our online presence is as much an expression of our Christian faith as any other aspect of our life.

A way forward

Online culture shock (the discovery that others do not agree with us or even like us) is likely to be a byproduct of a 'small-corner' offline life (which has probably shielded us from personal contact with those whose lives are very different from our own). It's time, though, to 'go out'.

- Think about online *and* offline arenas where you can connect with people you would not naturally journey through life with.

- Whatever you do, don't judge others; personal judgement is the Holy Spirit's task (John 16:8–9). Yours is to share what you know, even if it's not listened to (John 3:11), so get used to offering and answering rather than pronouncing or proclaiming (1 Peter 3:15).

God is light, and Christians are called to live in the light. Light protected in corners makes no difference to the wider darkness, and confirmation bias illuminates only what you want to see (even when it doesn't exist).

The biblical principle

> God is light; in him there is no darkness at all. If we claim to have fellowship with him and yet walk in the darkness, we lie and do not live out the truth. But if we walk in the light, as he is in the light, we have fellowship with one another, and the blood of Jesus, his Son, purifies us from all sin.
>
> 1 JOHN 1:5–7

- Some people are in darkness because they have not had the opportunity to understand the light (John 1:5).

- Others are in darkness because they do not wish to be seen (John 3:20).

The light of God, though, is personal, because Jesus is the light and so are his disciples, and God's light is always revealed person to person. There is no one brightness-illuminates-all impersonal light, and God's light does not dazzle, it reveals.

- Christians who interact with 'all guns blazing' fire off salvos of light that cause others to dive for cover.

- Christians who seek to control a 'spotlight of God' cause those caught in the beam to shield their eyes and look away.

- God's light is most powerfully revealed when Christians allow it to appropriately illuminate their own shortcomings and affirm how God has re-created them through Christ (1 John 1:8–9). If you are the light of the world (Matthew 5:14–16), the way *you* look at things is important, because your gaze illuminates.

Wisdom from the Psalms

Your word is a lamp for my feet,
a light on my path.
PSALM 119:105

Some questions to think about

1   Review your social media contacts. Are you in contact with anyone with whom you do not agree or who does not agree with you?

2   Consider the lumens (brightness) of your online and offline light. Is it so bright that anyone in darkness avoids it? Is it so dim that no one even notices it?

3   How can your church (or you as a parent) help children and young people to establish an appropriately balanced offline and online community life? What 'model' of community engagement is presented to them as the norm? What examples of non-confirmation-bias engagement are being lived out by the adults to whom they look for guidance?

18

Engaging the community

The way it is

In the UK, we commonly use the word 'community' in curious ways. 'Care in the community', for example, may describe housing provision for residents who are isolated from, and possibly even resented by, their neighbours – which begs the question, 'Where is the community within which these people are being cared for?' We also use 'community' to describe ethnic groups (maybe the 'Rubovian community' mentioned in Chapter 9). It can also describe the delivery of services (for example, nursing, home assistance, and so forth), and institutions where individuals have little choice but to be there (for example, schools). Even businesses are described as communities. If we tot up the number of different 'communities' within our geographical location, it will be a long list (and few will be linked to any others), and means that, for most British people, if they are part of a 'community' it will probably be relatively small and focused on a single interest. In contemporary Britain, 'community' does not so much resemble a Russian doll (community within community within community) as a Russian doll which has been taken apart and scattered.

Online interaction offers a means of connection in this disparate culture, but whether community is achieved will depend on the approach of those who use it. For example, technology offers an opportunity for the tech-generations to connect with one another in ways never before possible, but whether this opportunity is taken will depend on how each generation approaches their online life. For many families, the tech appears to divide, rather than unite (as each generation increasingly sticks to its own tech-culture). This division is not a by-product of the tech; it reflects the approach and flexibility (or lack of it) of the individuals concerned.

Communities are not abstract; they do not have an independent life of their own. Whether they are small (families) or large (neighbourhoods), they are created when individuals choose to contribute and commit to other people. They require personal effort, and they only exist when individuals make them happen.

'Connection' should not be confused with community. Connecting is just the equivalent of saying hello; if it is not followed up with contribution and commitment, the community is at best illusory, and at worst a means through which 'bad' people can abuse and manipulate 'good' people. The test for any online community is the same as for any offline community. It's the answer to this question: am I committed to and contributing to the needs of the other members of this community, just as they are committed to me and contributing to my needs? If the answer is no, then you are connected; if yes, then you are in a community.

In the UK, there are very few offline communities which include every generation, interest group and background. The church is one; but like any community, it does not just happen. Church communities are created when individuals contribute and commit to the well-being of the other members. The by-product is that those who focus on the needs of others belong.

Pause for thought

Some years ago, I knew a man whose community was his local pub. He socialised there every weekend, most midweek evenings, and lunchtime when he could. He was a lynchpin member of that community of regulars. Sadly, he fell ill and died, but his family were comforted knowing that the church would be packed for his funeral service. On the day, no one from the pub came, because what was thought of as his community were connected to the pub, not each other. Our contemporary, online communities have yet to be tested. Whether they are more than connection will be revealed as time goes on.

Digging deeper

Why do Christian people contribute and commit to the needs of others? Because in Christianity, the model of community is the community-within-community model:

- There is only one God, yet he is Father, Son and Holy Spirit (Deuteronomy 4:35; 2 Corinthians 13:14). God is a being and yet also a community of being.

- When creating human beings, God did not say, 'Let *me* make *you*,' but, 'Let *us* make *them*' (Genesis 1:26–27). God created human beings in his image; to be human is to be part of a created community which reflects God.

- Re-creation in Christ re-establishes inclusion within the household-community of God (Ephesians 2:12–19).

- The community nature of the church is expressed by individual Christians who commit to, and contribute to, the needs of other Christians (Acts 2:44–45).

- The church expresses its community nature to the wider community when it commits to, and contributes to, the needs of those beyond itself (Matthew 25:34–40).

Each expression of community, each 'inner doll', happens because of the 'doll' within which it sits; and all sit within the essential, 'outer doll' of the nature of God. Christianity is, by definition, a community faith, but if Christians are to engage in community life of any kind (whether it is with the local church community, or as the church with the wider community), it will be as a spiritual response – as individuals respond to God and focus on the needs of others.

Joining the dots

When Christians focus on their own needs, churches become places of division and difficulty (James 4:1–3). When Christians engage with God, their focus becomes him and then others (Matthew 22:37–39). This is true whether we interact offline or online – but it requires effort. Contact tends to come from a 'what I need' direction while community happens when we focus on God and others… which, to be honest, is just a very old truth expressed in a new vocabulary. So, let's revert to biblical terms. What you do and say reveals what is in your heart (Luke 6:43–45).

Be aware that, because communities require effort, if all three tech-generations are to be members of the same Christian community, they will have to work at it. For example, let's caricature something so simple that most people will expect it to happen effortlessly: how do you arrange a church committee meeting?

- If you are of the tech-immigrant generation, you agree it by letter, email, phone call or face-to-face. You write it in your pocket diary, or on your kitchen calendar. You prepare the papers needed in advance, take them with you and set off early to make sure that you are not late. You do this because your culture is offline. Without a mobile phone, tech or the internet, times and dates cannot be changed without massive organisational effort and, if you leave something important at home, you will not be able to go back and get it. You expect meetings to be occasions where ideas are aired for the first time, individual contributions are assessed and, after due consideration, final decisions are made. You will also expect social interaction – after all, you probably haven't seen the other committee members since the meeting was arranged!

- If you are of the tech-assimilator generation, you agree a meeting in advance, enter it in your 'digital diary' and rely on this to remind you where and when it is scheduled. Any documents you need will be accessible through your tablet or laptop, and while you may do some online research, time may defeat you, and you hope that others in the meeting won't notice you reading the relevant papers as it progresses. If the time or location of the meeting changes, you will be irritated but you will cope, and you expect to either make decisions or to be given direction for further thought and exploration in order to reach a decision in a future meeting. You do this because, although your culture is primarily offline, you have assimilated online tools which help you to function in your offline culture.

- If you are of the tech-indigenous generation, you expect to know in advance on which morning, afternoon or evening the meeting will take place, and you enter that in your phone app. Nearer to the time, someone will establish a time, so you enter that too and rearrange any conflicts that now arise. It will not concern you if you do not know, until you are en route, the location of the meeting (after all, you know the neighbourhood; the exact address is merely a detail), and if you are late it doesn't matter because you have already discussed a good deal of the agenda with other tech-indigenous colleagues online in, around and among your other digital networks. The meeting itself exists primarily to ask a few questions and rubber-stamp what has already been decided. You do this because, in your online culture, little happens in blocks of time or in specific locations, but in small packets of time when you are elsewhere doing other things. The one thing you don't expect to do is socialise – after all, you socialise online with other committee members continually.

So, there's a caricature of the three tech-generations – but do you recognise yourself and others? How are you going to build a church community when the simple act of arranging a meeting can end in misunderstanding, frustration and bubbling anger? And if building a church community is challenging, how can a church impact the wider community? The answer is easy to say but hard to do: building any community not only requires hard work but a willingness to be cross-cultural (Romans 12:16; 1 Corinthians 1:10). The key is to be aware of your differences and culture, but to focus on God and on others (Romans 16:17).

A way forward

Twenty-first century British culture is individualistic, but individuals yearn for community... provided they can be included on *their* terms (that's individualism!). That kind of community, however, does not exist. Unless individuals commit and contribute (in other words, give up elements of their individuality for the sake of the community), no community comes into being. Similarly, unless individual contributions and commitment are sustained, communities die.

Because of who God is, because of what Christ has done, and because of the presence of the Holy Spirit, the church is a community. It's what so many yearn for – so why are vast numbers not even looking in the church's direction?

- One possible answer is that, both offline and online, Christians are broadcasting arguments rather than proclaiming the God who unites (Romans 14:1). The message being disseminated is 'Christians are people who fight', rather than 'Christians are people who love' (1 Corinthians 13:4–7).

- Christians behaving badly is nothing new. Try reading 1 Corinthians, but concentrate on the issues Paul was addressing, and ask, 'Is this a church I'd like to join?' (I know *my* answer... I'd rather stick forks in my eyes...) When others look at the offline and online community of your church, or read your online opinions about your church, your faith and God, do they see a church and faith they'd like to join?

To quote a host of singers and pop bands who have covered the same song, 'It ain't what you do; it's the way that you do it.' When you log on, what is in your heart? When Christians interact (offline or online) intentionally and prayerfully, their contributions become useful and used by those who are seeking direction and, for those who are looking, there's the opportunity for them to look beyond the interaction to the living God. It's at this point that your faith, and the church community to which you are committed and contribute, begins to make sense to the wider community.

If you are engaging with a community of any kind (your family, your church, your neighbourhood, offline or online), if you are a Christian, your community engagement will rest within your engagement with God.

The biblical principle

> Rejoice with those who rejoice; mourn with those who mourn. Live in harmony with one another. Do not be proud, but be willing to associate with people of low position. Do not be conceited.
> ROMANS 12:15–16

People judge how genuine faith is not by the words proclaimed, but by the clear, congruent connection between words said and deeds done – because that indicates the intentions of the heart (James 2:15–17). When someone is in trouble, messages arrive on their social media page proclaiming, 'I'm there for you!' Is that community or contact? If it's pixels on a screen, it's contact. If it's words backed by commitment and contribution, it's community.

What would Jesus post?

What will you post?

Wisdom from the Psalms

> May these words of my mouth and this meditation of my heart
>   be pleasing in your sight,
>   Lord, my Rock and my Redeemer.
>
> PSALM 19:14

Some questions to think about

1 When you think about your church, what immediately comes to mind? If your list does not begin with 'God and others', what does this reveal about your approach to church?

2 What, in your church, takes the most time and effort? Does it build community?

3 What, in your neighbourhood, needs the most time and effort? Is your church committed and contributing?

4 Make a list of offline and online church responsibilities, and work out who fulfils them and which tech-generation they come from. Where do your tech-indigenous generation members feature on your list? What does this reveal?

Conclusion

The way it is

The technological complexity of computer software and internet-ready devices can seem dauntingly futuristic, and online interaction incredibly modern, but what is achieved is ancient: people communicating with each other. Some regard their online life as a tool, others as a distraction, yet others as a game where their aim is to play a role as a self-created avatar quite other from their offline self. How you approach online interaction will depend in part on which tech-generation you come from. Some will ask, 'Is the internet really that important?' Leaving aside the fact that only someone from the tech-immigrant generation would ask that, consider the facts:

- In the UK, broadband speed is now a factor in where people decide to live.

- In the developing world, access to the internet is a factor in young people transitioning to city life (there is no wifi on the family farm).

You may not think that the internet is important to *you*, but that is not the same as the internet not being important… and if you are a Christian, you are concerned about the needs of others.

Take, as a final example, the growing 'gig economy'. In the offline past, work was regulated by contracts of employment. In the transitioning offline-online recent past, 'zero-hours' contracts attempted to address the needs of those who worked casually. These contracts have been used by some employers to treat workers badly, but they are paradise compared to the online 'gig-economy'. This is payment for task achieved, not hours worked, and it's the basis of most new taxi, delivery and task-based companies. Workers are managed by a computer program, so they log on (ready to work) and their phone app tells them where to go and what to do. When the task is finished, it tells them what to do next – and the app decides how much pay they will receive for *each gig* as it takes into account how much each customer is willing to pay (which it knows through their purchase data) and how much the worker will accept without quitting (ditto). Not only do gig-workers have no guaranteed employment or rights, they often receive less than the minimum wage.

So, is that online interaction important? You may not be a gig-worker, but people in your neighbourhood are, and maybe some are even in your church? When you discover their situation, what will you offer? A biblical approach?

Digging deeper

This book asks the question, 'What would Jesus post?' If we think that question refers to the incarnate Christ sitting down at a keyboard 2,000 years ago, the answer is likely to be, 'We don't know!' If, however, we think of the church as the body of Christ, with Jesus as the head and Christians as the body parts (Ephesians 5:23b), then we are his hands, feet, ears and voice. This means that our posts (like our words and deeds) are also Christ's. So, if you want to know what Jesus *is* posting, read the posts of Christians; that's what his body is posting and one would expect his body to be connected to his head. Of course, if you read these posts and mutter, 'Um, this doesn't sound much like Jesus!', it suggests that there is a disconnection between head and body.

The starting place is not what others do, though, it's what *you* do. Online interaction is now part of everyday life, and there are biblical principles for communicating with fellow believers, with those of little or different faiths, with those who violently disagree – in fact with pretty much everyone. Revisit those biblical principles and let the Holy Spirit guide you as you apply them in a digital age.

Joining the dots

In this book, we have considered: the internet as a public arena, prayer, porn, confession, sowing seeds, our digital tongue, dwelling in God's presence, wisdom and discernment, humility, hospitality and generosity, the sabbath, spiritual gifts, spiritual fruit, gossip, persecution, the footprints we leave and community. This book, however, is not all-encompassing; it addresses a selection of issues and the focus is on the Christian stewardship of personal online interactions. Neither is this book a comprehensive manual to apply (as a Pharisee would), or a book of rules (as some religions offer). It's a place to begin, a direction in which to think and an encouragement to rely on our relationship with God as we further relationships with others by interacting online. We all constantly get relationships wrong, but every time we fall flat on our faces, God picks us up, dusts us off, and asks; 'Ready for another go? Try looking at me this time…'

There is a common secular phrase which says, 'Life is what you make it.' For Christians, that phrase, like every aspect of life, is changed to, 'My life is what God makes it.' When it comes to our online interactions, our expectations are no different, and if we approach them biblically, they become what God makes them.

Pause for thought

Many people find Jesus' parable of the shrewd manager (Luke 16:1–9) baffling, but Jesus is just pointing out that dishonest people reap worldly rewards and that 'people of the light' behave differently. In a digital age, if you join the online scrum and put the boot in, everyone will be your friend. If you pursue online self-interest, your bank balance will bulge. If you abuse and ridicule others, you will be celebrated. It's the same old choice, though – be applauded by the world, or by God. That's up to you... unless you follow Jesus. Then, it's up to him (John 15:18–27).

A way forward

One of the teachers of the law... asked [Jesus], 'Of all the commandments, which is the most important?' 'The most important one,' answered Jesus, 'is this: "Hear, O Israel: The Lord our God, the Lord is one. Love the Lord your God with all your heart and with all your soul and with all your mind and with all your strength." The second is this: "Love your neighbour as yourself."'

MARK 12:28–31a

- The teacher wanted to be told what to do. He wanted an action plan.

- Jesus pointed him to the core principle, which is love, and expected the man to work it out from there (if he was really interested). And, you can almost hear Jesus' unspoken question, 'Would you like to come with me and find out more?'

- That's how Jesus operated then, and it's how he operates now. Unless we keep close to Jesus, none of us has a chance of working anything much out, at all!

The biblical principle

If any of you lacks wisdom, you should ask God, who gives generously to all without finding fault, and it will be given to you.

JAMES 1:5

Let's revisit the question asked right at the start of this book. Why would any 21st-century person seek to approach their online interactions biblically? Because, it is as we interact with Jesus, through the Holy Spirit, that God changes us into world-changers (John 17:15–21).

Wisdom from the Psalms

Give praise to the Lord, proclaim his name;
    make known among the nations what he has done.
Sing to him, sing praise to him;
    tell of all his wonderful acts.
Glory in his holy name;
    let the hearts of those who seek the Lord rejoice.
Look to the Lord and his strength;
    seek his face always.

PSALM 105:1–4

Some questions to think about

1 At the beginning of this book, you were asked, 'What is your hope for your online life?' At the end of this book, ask that question again and compare your answers. Has anything changed?

2 If your answers are the same, does this indicate 'application issues'? What practical steps can you take to help you put into practice what you know in your head?

3 If your answers are different, what is the key shift in your understanding?

Afterword

I was born in the tech-immigrant generation, and have always been a tech-assimilator but will never be tech-indigenous. I use a pocket diary, make notes on random sheets of paper (which I keep in piles), and prefer a wristwatch with hands. I use a desktop computer with two screens for work, two laptops for personal projects, a mini-tablet for games (and for checking my five different email accounts), and I leave my two-sim phone on silent so often that I forget to look at it.

As a British Christian, I'm like a first-century Gentile convert. Neither Christianity nor church figured in my childhood, but when, as a teenager, I first understood that Jesus Christ had offered his life for me, I offered mine back. From that moment on, perhaps like Titus, I received the letters of Paul (and the rest of the Bible), and asked two fundamental questions: 'How do I live this new-creation life in my own time and culture?' and, when thinking about the broader issues of life, 'How do I approach them biblically?' All of my writing is driven by my desire to find, if not answers, Christ-focused directions in which to travel. This book is no exception.

I am not a tech-expert and if you land on my website (or any of my four social media pages), you will meet someone who does some things well and others poorly. If you dig below my ideas and meet me as a person, you will find someone seeking to live for Christ, who often gets it wrong and has to confess and apologise – and someone who may even have forgotten a key biblical insight that he, himself, shared with everyone else! In short, I am a Christian in a relationship with the living God who is made known through Christ.

What Would Jesus Post? is neither an attempt to cover all possible biblical principles nor a one-stop guide to every online issue. I (and the church of which I am vicar) will be working through the issues highlighted in this book – just like you! I think of this book as a place to begin, to reflect on the shared experience of online life (and its implications) and to ask, 'How can Christians approach online life biblically?' And I think that asking that question frequently will be more productive than seeking a final, all-encompassing answer.

Notes

1 Laura Treneer, *Church Online: Social Media* (BRF, 2017) and *Church Online: Websites* (BRF, 2017).

2 Bible references include letters ('a' or 'b'). These indicate the first or second half of a verse.

3 David Robertson, *Marriage: Restoring our vision* (BRF, 2005; reprinted Parbar Publishing, 2012).

4 Charles M. Sheldon, *In His Steps: What would Jesus do?* (Hurst & Company, 1896).

5 Treneer, *Church Online: Social Media* and *Church Online: Websites*.

6 Laura Treneer, *Church from the Inside* (BRF, 2017) and *Church from the Outside* (BRF, 2017).

7 Gordon Murray, 'A Rubovian Legend' (youtube.com/watch?v=F9XHQE7satc).

8 Adam Curtis, 'The power of nightmares' (archive.org/details/ThePowerOfNightmares-AdamCurtis).

9 David Robertson, *Collaborative Ministry: What it is, how it works and why* (BRF, 2007; revised edition, Parbar Publishing 2016), Chapter 10.

10 Izabella Kominska, *The Financial Times*; Presenter: Jaques Perretti, 'Billion dollar deals and how they changed your world' (BBC2, Series 1, Episode 2; first broadcast October 2017).

11 Kominska, *The Financial Times*.

12 Susan B. Warner, 'Jesus bids us shine' (Edwin O. Excell, 1884).

Engaging the Word will transform the Bible engagement habits of Christian disciples, improving the health of the church by opening up new opportunities for drawing on God's word and new life as a result. This book sets out what biblical literacy means and what it looks like in our contemporary culture, exploring the benefits of biblical literacy for those who follow Jesus and for Christian leaders as local theologians and preachers. It also presents a series of practical explorations of the role of the Bible, which help us to reach up to God, reach in to develop our own identity in Christ and reach out to others.

Engaging the Word
Biblical literacy and Christian discipleship
Peter M. Phillips
978 0 85746 583 2 £7.99

brfonline.org.uk

musings of a clergy child
growing into a faith of my own

Nell Goddard

Vicarage life can be exciting, hilarious, scary, surreal and delightful... and that's just one day! Nell Goddard writes honestly and openly about the ins and outs of growing up in a Christian home, from her experience as the daughter of two vicars. With hilarious anecdotes, tough lessons and spiritual reflections from wrestling with faith, this book charts what it's like to live in the goldfish bowl of a vicarage, grow up in the shadow of your parents, lose your faith and find it again.

Musings of a Clergy Child
Growing into a faith of my own
Nell Goddard
978 0 85746 546 7 £7.99

brfonline.org.uk

BRF

Transforming
lives and communities

Christian growth and understanding of the Bible

Resourcing individuals, groups and leaders in churches for their own spiritual journey and for their ministry

Church outreach in the local community

Offering three programmes that churches are embracing to great effect as they seek to engage with their local communities and transform lives

Teaching Christianity in primary schools

Working with children and teachers to explore Christianity creatively and confidently

Children's and family ministry

Working with churches and families to explore Christianity creatively and bring the Bible alive

Visit **brf.org.uk** for more information on BRF's work

brf.org.uk

The Bible Reading Fellowship (BRF) is a Registered Charity (No. 233280)